THE Millionaire KIT $

SURPRISINGLY SIMPLE STRATEGIES FOR BUILDING REAL WEALTH

STEPHEN L. NELSON

TIMES BUSINESS

RANDOM HOUSE

In the preparation of this book, every effort has been made to offer the most current, correct, and clearly expressed information possible. Nonetheless, inadvertent errors can occur and rules and regulations governing personal finance and investing often change. Further, the application and impact of investment rules and laws can vary widely from case to case based upon the unique facts involved. Consequently, the author and publisher specifically disclaim any liability or loss that is incurred as a consequence of the use and application, directly or indirectly, of any information presented in this book. If legal advice or other expert assistance is required, the services of a professional should be sought.

Copyright © 1998 by Stephen L. Nelson, Inc.

All rights reserved under International and Pan-American Copyright Conventions. Published in the United States by Times Books, a division of Random House, Inc., New York, and simultaneously in Canada by Random House of Canada Limited, Toronto.

Library of Congress Cataloging-in-Publication Data

Nelson, Stephen L.
The millionaire kit : surprisingly simple strategies for building real wealth /
Stephen L. Nelson — 1st ed.
p.   cm.
ISBN 0-8129-3004-5 (alk. paper)
1. Finance, Personal. I. Title.
HG179.N42616   1998
332.024—dc21   98-16182

Book design by Anne Scatto / PIXEL PRESS

Random House website address: www.randomhouse.com
Printed in the United States of America on acid-free paper

9   8   7   6   5   4   3   2

FIRST EDITION

Acknowledgments

A book typically represents a collaboration. Many talented people contribute energy, enthusiasm, and good ideas. *The Millionaire Kit,* predictably, is no exception. Many friends and colleagues shared their insights, comments, and criticism. My agent, Claudette Moore, of the Moore Literary Agency, convinced me to turn the Millionaire Kit formula into a book. Tracy Smith, my editor at Times Books/Random House, helped expand the applicability of the Millionaire Kit's tools and strategies so they let just about anyone build real wealth. Luke Mitchell, my other editor, ably took over for Tracy when she left to have a baby, and kept the project rolling along. Jeff Adell, programmer extraordinaire, bullet-proofed the Millionaire Maker software tools. Kaarin Dolliver, a co-worker, checked facts, tested the software, and offered constructive comments. Eric Wuhrley, a Ph.D. candidate in finance at the University of Washington, double-checked the facts and software calculations. Jim Brown of Microsoft Press, Carla Bayha of Borders, and Mike Ferrari of Barnes & Noble enthusiastically supported the Millionaire Kit in a bunch of indirect ways because they thought it was a cool tool for readers.

Finally, I want to point out that without Carie Freimuth and Peter Bernstein, respectively the associate publisher and publisher of Times Books, this book would never have been published. They saw the unique value of this unusual book and figured out how to make everything work.

Contents

Read Me First

I need to start this book with a qualification and then the clarification.

Here's the qualification: I don't believe that you will live a happier, more fulfilling, more exciting life if you're wealthy. I've spent almost all of my adult life advising people about their money or writing about how people can better manage their money. And though I've worked and talked with many wealthy people, I have never seen nor heard of any evidence—even anecdotal or secondhand—that the rich automatically get more out of life, enjoy better marriages, or for some wealth-related reason experience something that most people miss. The old adage "Money doesn't buy happiness" is true. And I suspect you know this.

But—and this is an important but—I do think that financial independence and financial security produce peace of mind. People who are wealthy can avoid much of the financial stress that most of their neighbors and friends bear. For someone who's wealthy, a broken car is an annoyance and not a crisis. For someone who's wealthy, a child's entrance into college is cause for celebration, not consternation. For someone who's wealthy, looming macroeconomic problems like a bankrupt Medicare trust fund or the Social Security debacle matter politically and are something to be considered while participating in our democracy, but they don't really matter personally. The wealthy person really doesn't need to worry how they'll affect his or her pocketbook.

I also need to make an important clarification before I go any further. This book isn't about materialism or greed. This book is really about financial balance. While the notion of financial balance may seem strange to you—especially if you view wealth or the wealthy with suspicion—I stand by my statement. By working toward financial independence, you effectively set aside money from your bountiful years so that you more easily get through the lean years. By achieving financial independence, you effectively apportion your income over the years you and your family spend—using, for example, thirty years of wages to pay for sixty years of living. If these benefits sound immoral or unethical to you, you need to be honest about the alternatives: By not working toward financial independence, minor financial mishaps easily turn into personal or family catastrophes. By not achieving financial independence, you commit yourself either to working until the day you die or old-age poverty.

For these reasons, this book describes—without embarrassment or apology—how you accumulate wealth. You will use the information and software tools provided as part of this book to become financially independent—even a millionaire if you want.

HOW THIS BOOK WORKS

What the Millionaire Kit does is pretty simple. The Millionaire Kit just describes a strategy that almost anyone can use to accumulate wealth and thereby achieve financial independence, and it provides the software programs necessary for implementing the strategy.

One really important thing for you to understand is that both the strategy and the software are simple. The strategy is simple to understand, prove, and use. And the software is simple to use if you know how Microsoft Windows or the Apple Macintosh works. If you don't know how they work, you can just refer to Appendix A, "Using the Millionaire Maker Software."

SOME FINAL QUICK COMMENTS

You may have already guessed this, but you use this book just like you use any other book. You begin your reading with the first chapter, and then continue on from there. The only thing that's really different is that occasionally, usually just two or three times a chapter, you will see a boxed note that looks something like this:

Insight

Use the **EASY LOAN COMPARER** from the companion CD to accurately determine which loan alternative costs you the least money. To do this, follow these steps:

STEP 1   Start the Easy Loan Comparer in the same manner as you start any Windows or Macintosh program.

STEP 2   Enter the amount you plan to borrow into the **Loan amount** box.

STEP 3   Enter the number of years it will take to repay the loan into the **Loan repayment term in years** box.

STEP 4   For each loan alternative, supply the loan's annual interest rate and the total fees by entering these values into the appropriate boxes. For example, use the **Loan #1 Annual interest rate** box and the **Loan #1 Total loan fees** box for the first loan alternative you're considering.

STEP 5   Click the **Estimate** button, and the Easy Loan Comparer calculates the monthly payment, effective interest rate, total payments, and total costs for each of the loans you're considering. The loan alternative that shows the lowest effective annual percentage rate represents the cheapest loan.

STEP 6   Optionally, click the **Print** button to print a copy of your loan comparison results.

This boxed note alerts you to a software tool from the companion disk that you can use to think more intelligently about some financial issue, make a financial decision, or ponder a financial trade-off.

I need to make one other comment before we get started. When someone does computer-based financial modeling—which is what you're doing when you use any of the Millionaire Kit software programs—one is sorely tempted to let personal biases creep into the modeling. And these personal biases can greatly distort the accuracy of your estimates.

Unfortunately, there isn't to my knowledge a bunch of good, empirical data that backs up this point. But over the almost two decades that I've been performing computer-based financial modeling, I've noticed two strange things.

For one, if you're someone who's a bit of a pessimist, someone who maybe sees a half glass of milk as half empty, your personality affects your modeling in all sorts of little ways. If you're trying to guess how inflation will affect your investments, for example, you are perhaps more likely to use inflation rates higher than you should. If you're trying to estimate the future value of some investment, you are more likely to use annual rates of returns lower than you should. You're also more likely, in my experience, to find mistakes or modeling errors that overstate positive results than you are to find mistakes or modeling errors that overstate negative results. To sum things up, if you are a conservative, cautious, and perhaps slightly pessimistic person, it can affect the calculations you perform in a bunch of little ways. This doesn't seem like all that big a deal. But it can be because when you combine all the little ways your personality affects your calculations, the combination ends up having a big effect.

The same characteristic, not surprisingly, tends to infect people who are upbeat, aggressive optimists, too. In my experience, if you're like this, you're much more likely to use inflation rates that are too low and annual rates of returns that are a bit too high. I also think you're more likely to find mistakes and modeling errors that understate positive results than you are to find mistakes or modeling errors that overstate positive results.

Okay, now I can guess what you're thinking. You're saying, "How much difference can a handful of small differences make?" Well, you see, that's the problem. If you're a little off here and a little off there, in the end you can find your calculation results greatly affected.

I don't mean to throw you right into complicated financial calculations, but this is really important for you to understand. So, stay with me here and take the simple case of two twenty-five-year-olds—Joe Pessimist and Jane Optimist—forecasting the value they will have in their individual retirement accounts (IRAs) when they retire at age sixty-five after contributing $2,000 a year. Let's also suppose that they both invest in a stock mutual fund.

Here's how Joe Pessimist might figure things. Perhaps he would use an 8.8 percent rate of return for figuring the annual gross return of the fund because that's the long-term rate of return on the U.S. stock market since just after the American Civil War. Maybe Joe would also use a 4 percent inflation rate because even though inflation since the Civil War has been right around 2.3 percent, inflation in this century has run around 3.5 percent and he figures it'll make sense to just round up. And then let's say that Mr. Pessimist also figures on a 1 percent annual expense ratio because that's close to the average expense ratio charged by stock mutual funds. An expense ratio just shows how much of your return you give up to the mutual fund to pay for its operating expenses.

Using these inputs, Joe forecasts that he will accumulate roughly $230,000, adjusting for inflation, by age sixty-five. Which is a reasonable, albeit very conservative, forecast.

Now here's how Jane Optimist might figure things for essentially the same situation. Jane might use the roughly seventy-year average stock market return, which is just over 10 percent. But then she might decide to use the really long-term inflation rate of 2.3 percent and round down to 2 percent. Finally, Ms. Optimist might use a 0.2 percent expense ratio because she notes that the stock mutual fund both she and Joe use actually charges a low, 0.2 percent expense ratio.

Using these inputs, Jane—assuming she makes no mistakes—might forecast that she will accumulate $518,000, again adjusting for inflation, by age sixty-five. Which is another reasonable forecast. Although I should point out that the weakest part of this forecast concerns the inflation rate. The reason that inflation since the American Civil War averages just over 2 percent is that there was a period of painful deflation in the last part of the nineteenth century. Inflation between 1872 and 1925, in fact, averaged only 1.2 percent annually.

But now you see how large the difference can be, right? It's huge. The pessimist thinks he's going to end up with $230,000, while the optimist thinks she's going to end up with more than twice that amount, or $518,000. And the difference stems from a handful of minor changes in inputs.

The bottom line—and the reason why it's really important for you to consider this point—is that your personality will affect your use of the software programs in surprisingly large ways.

Okay, what should you do about this? You want to do a handful of things. First off, you want to make sure that you've entered your inputs correctly. You want to try a calculation more than once. If you can, it's great to review your inputs and calculations with other people who understand what you're doing. This review increases the chance that you'll catch more of your errors.

Another thing you want to do is perform "sensitivity analysis." Sensitivity analysis just means that you try a calculation with more than one set of inputs. Try different inflation rates, for example. Try varying annual rates of return. In particular, consider your own personality quirks and force yourself to experiment with input variables beyond the range in which you feel comfortable. For the obvious reason, optimists should force themselves to work with input variables that are conservative, cautious, and terribly pessimistic. Pessimists should force themselves to work with input variables that are pie in the sky, aggressive, ridiculously optimistic. What you want to do with sensitivity analysis is get some sort of gut feel about how much your calculation results change when you change input variables. Usually, with compound interest calculations, they change a lot. You also want to make sure that you keep your eyes open to the complete range of possibilities.

A third and final tactic I'd suggest is that, where practical, you talk with other people about the input variables they expect. This maybe sounds funny, but surprising numbers of investors, including other readers of this book, are thinking about appropriate inflation rates and sustainable annual rates of return. If you consider the reasons why the person who works in the cubicle next to yours is using a 5 percent inflation rate, you'll probably be smarter about setting inflation rates for your calculations. If you hear why your neighbor thinks she can earn only 8 percent annually, you'll be more clever about estimating returns in your calculations. This isn't to say that you should rely on any old Tom, Dick, or Harriet's economic views. If you're the sort of person who reads a book like this, my guess is you've got your head screwed on a lot straighter than the average man or woman on the street. But by considering different points of view, you'll almost certainly think more clearly about things like investing, inflation, and long-term prospects of the economy.

Let me mention one final thing about the personality bias business. I suspect that if you're a pessimist, you'll probably end up in better financial shape than you think you will. That's the almost inevitable result of always conservatively estimating outcomes. And then, conversely, if you're an optimist, I think you'll probably always end up in worse shape than you think you will.

I'm not sure how you should use this information. And perhaps it's bold of me to call it information. But reflect on it a bit. Pessimists may correctly conclude they don't need to worry as much as they do. And optimists may fairly decide they need to build in a little additional financial cushion in their plans.

And now we're finally ready to begin.

Chapter

1

THE MILLIONAIRE KIT FORMULA

One of the reasons that many of the settlers of the American West experienced the disasters they did is that they knew only in which direction they wanted to go: west. They really didn't understand the specific route—which road, river, mountain pass, and so forth—they needed to take. As a result, small wagon trains that included pregnant women and small children attempted routes that would challenge, and might defeat, an adult on horseback or, for that matter, one in a sport utility vehicle. And the predictable result was that many of these settlers, the ones who knew the direction but not a real route, never made it to where they wanted.

This difference between a direction and route applies in many areas—not the least of which is financial planning. So, the very first thing you need to understand about wealth is that there are, for all practical purposes, only three routes to wealth: instant wealth, entrepreneurial wealth, and investment wealth. It's useful to look at all three—and to understand them. If you're truly going to become wealthy, you'll need to take one of these routes.

INSTANT WEALTH

Let's start off by describing instant wealth. Instant wealth comes from a variety of sources. The lottery (a big one). An inheritance from your rich aunt—the one who never had any kids of her own because she was so busy making money. An overnight killing in the commodities market. You read the newspaper—you've heard the stories, right?

The problem with the instant wealth route is that it doesn't really work, or at least not as a general solution. State lotteries really amount to a tax on the naïve. Millions play, but few win. In fact, contestants spend more money on postage entering those play-by-mail sweepstakes than the sponsor gives away in prizes.

 Insight

Use the LOTTERY CALCULATOR from the companion CD to see how many times you need to play a lottery to win:

STEP 1   Start the Lottery Calculator in the same manner as you start any Windows or Macintosh program.

STEP 2   Enter the amount a winning lottery ticket will pay into the **Lottery total payoff** box. This box initially holds the value $1,000,000, but you can replace this by typing a replacement value.

STEP 3   Enter the cost of one lottery ticket into the **Cost of ticket** box. (This box initially holds the value $1.00, but you can replace this by typing a replacement value.)

STEP 4   Enter the six winning lottery numbers you think will be drawn into the **Enter your numbers** boxes.

Insight (continued)

STEP 5   Click the **Play Once** button to play the lottery one time, which is equivalent to buying one ticket.

STEP 6   Click the **Play 100** button to play the lottery a hundred times, which is equivalent to buying a hundred tickets.

STEP 7   Click the **Play 1000** button to play the lottery 1,000 times, which is equivalent to buying 1,000 tickets.

STEP 8   Optionally, click the **Example** button to have the Lottery Calculator randomly select six lottery numbers and then purchase a single ticket.

STEP 9   Optionally, click the **Print** button to print a copy of your calculation results. Note, by the way, that the calculator tallies your total winnings and total ticket purchases for all the times you've played the lottery since starting the Lottery Calculator.

Most of us don't have rich aunts. And even if we do, we can never be sure that we'll actually get an inheritance—even if we're in the will today. Estate taxes and rival heirs almost always successfully dissipate large estates.

And then this idea that you can take, for example, $1,000 and turn it into $100,000 in some relatively short time frame is of no practical value. As we'll discuss in the next chapter, "Six Principles of Simple Investing," any investment that might conceivably produce this sort of phenomenal return requires, by its very nature, that you bear phenomenal risk. And this risk means that perhaps nine out of ten times or ninety-nine out of a hundred times, you lose your investment rather than make a profit.

Because instant wealth isn't a practical route to wealth—attempting the instant wealth route usually prevents you from accumulating wealth—this book doesn't talk about the instant wealth route.

ENTREPRENEURIAL WEALTH

Entrepreneurial wealth represents a second route to riches. And, to be very honest, the entrepreneurial wealth route does work. In fact, entrepreneurial wealth is really the only way to accumulate a monstrous amount of money. By "monstrous," I don't mean a few hundred thousand dollars or even a few million dollars but rather tens of millions or hundreds of millions of dollars.

We've all heard the stories. A couple of bright kids build some neat product. Perhaps one that uses some newfangled technology. People want the product and so, seemingly overnight, these young entrepreneurs have a growing business. Over a period of years, they plow their profits back into the business. Fifteen or twenty years go by. And then the entrepreneurs, now typically middle-aged men, become superrich because of the value of the company they founded and grew.

Like I said, you've heard the stories. And you very probably know of or vaguely remember the entrepreneurial successes of William Hewlett and David Packard, founders of Hewlett-Packard Company; Steve Jobs and Steve Wozniak, founders of Apple Computer; and Bill Gates and Paul Allen, founders of Microsoft.

I don't want to discourage you from pursuing the entrepreneurial route to wealth. Nevertheless, I also don't think the entrepreneurial route is the one that most people should take. Sure, the entrepreneurial route may lead you to more wealth. But entrepreneurial wealth requires more risk taking. It makes you bear more stress. And to succeed, in my observation, you need to possess the right sort of personality. Interestingly, data suggest that most entrepreneurs feel this same way, too. Entrepreneurs typically don't encourage their children, for example, to follow in their footsteps. Instead, they often encourage sons and daughters to do something else with their lives—like enter a profession.

Besides all of this, there's an easier and more surefooted route to wealth, and I'll describe it next.

INVESTMENT WEALTH

So what's the third and most practical route to wealth? Investment wealth. Here's the deal: If you regularly invest some reasonable percentage of your income—and you're smart in your investing—you can accumulate substantial wealth. This isn't a trick. It's not some flaky get-rich-quick scheme. And it's not something that financial experts ever disagree about. The investment wealth route works because it's based on a mathematical reality called compound interest.

 **Insight**

Use the **INVESTMENT CALCULATOR** from the companion CD to see how much you will accumulate in an investment portfolio over, say, twenty-five years if you stash away $100 a month and earn 10 percent annually. To do this, follow these steps:

STEP 1 Start the Investment Calculator in the same manner as you start any Windows or Macintosh program.

STEP 2 Mark the **Future balance** button to identify the investment variable you want to calculate.

STEP 3 Mark the **monthly** button to identify how often you'll save additional amounts.

STEP 4 Enter 0 into the **Initial investment balance** box, since we'll assume you start with zero savings.

STEP 5 Enter 25 into the **Investment term** box to specify the years you'll save.

STEP 6 Enter 10 into the **Annual return on investment** box.

Insight (continued)

STEP 7   Enter 100 into the **Regular investment addition** box.

STEP 8   Click the **Estimate** button, and the Investment Calculator calculates the estimated wealth amount, placing the result in the **Future investment balance** box.

STEP 9   Optionally, click the **Print** button to print a copy of your calculation results.

HOW THIS BOOK APPLIES THE INVESTMENT WEALTH APPROACH

Now don't stop reading. I can guess what you're thinking at this point. Either you think you don't have the extra $100 or whatever to invest each month or you think that you don't have twenty-five years or whatever to wait. But I think you can find the money. And almost everybody has the time.

Let's talk about the problem of finding the money first. You're right that it's tough to find extra money to save. But what you may not know is that a major portion of the money you'll need—perhaps even most of it—can come from someone else. It's very likely that if you need $100 each month for an investment wealth program, for example, you can get much of the $100 from somebody else. It's not going to come out of your grocery budget, for example. And you're not going to have to move into quarters half the size of your current home.

One other thing: If you're smarter about the big financial decisions that you will make from this point forward, you'll almost surely find all of the other money you need to create investment wealth. And I don't mean to say that you've been making dumb decisions to date—or that every decision you make from this point forward needs to be perfect. No. What I really mean is that if you make smart decisions in a handful of big areas—by using the strategies described in this book and by using the soft-ware programs on the companion CD—you should be able to achieve financial independence.

Don't get discouraged, either, just because you're older. For goodness sake, don't assume that you can't run the program described here unless you have twenty-five or thirty years. Many, perhaps most baby boomers can jump-start their investment wealth programs by taking advantage of or even by creating a financial windfall opportunity.

To reiterate, the Millionaire Kit describes how just about anyone can achieve financial independence using an investment wealth program. The Kit explains how you can get the money you need from other people and from a handful of smart money decisions. And, for people who don't have a couple of decades to wait, the Kit tells you how to jump-start your investment wealth program and thereby accelerate your journey to finan-cial independence.

I don't want to beat a dead horse here, but let me give you three quick examples of how a clever decision or two combined with the strategies described in this book can produce a huge amount of wealth:

- If a twenty-five-year-old pack-a-day smoker quits and puts his cigarette money (about $1,000 a year) into an individual retirement account, he'll actually be able to save between $1,300 and $1,800 a year because of extra tax savings. This amount varies because the extra tax savings he gets by making the IRA contribution depends on his income. If this ex-smoker makes the IRA contribution over the forty years he'll presumably work, he will accumulate between $260,000 and $364,000 in present-day, uninflated dollars by age sixty-five. These amounts should rather easily produce financial independence for the ex-smoker.

- If a thirty-something married couple together making $50,000 applies a handful of the free-money ideas from Chapters 3, 4, and 5, they might easily find themselves with an extra and truly painless $200 a month for savings. By investing this amount into an employer's 401(k) plan, they would probably be able to save about $4,000 a year. The $200 a month grows to $4,000 a year because of employer matching and tax savings. Over thirty years, this couple's 401(k) plan would grow to roughly $378,000 in present-day, uninflated dollars. This amount—which, remember, the couple can accumulate painlessly—should produce financial independence.

- A fifty-year-old self-employed consultant making, say, $100,000 a year might be able to apply the strategies from Chapters 3, 4, 5, and 6 and come up with $10,000 a year, which would actually let her contribute about $15,000 to a special type of IRA available for self-employed individuals. The $10,000 grows to $15,000 in this case because of the income tax savings. If this woman could jump-start her investment wealth program with a $100,000 windfall (she could probably do this by applying one of the strategies explained in Chapter 6), she would end up with around $500,000 after twelve years and almost $700,000 after fifteen years.

These are just a few examples. But they should give you a feel for just what's possible. The plan that this book touts works for people who are young and for people who are older. It works for people with modest incomes and for people who make lots of money. It works for employees as well as the self-employed. Predictably, the plan doesn't work in exactly the same way for everybody. What works for a single twenty-five-year-old making, say, $20,000 differs from what works for a middle-class family making $50,000 and from what works for a high-income, self-employed fifty-year-old. But the core principles are the same. An investment wealth program works if you give it time, and you can painlessly find the money you need to fund the plan by using your computer and the software tools on the companion CD.

Let me make one final general observation about the investment wealth program described in this book: The program described here doesn't require you to turn into a financial genius or become a highly disciplined accountant. As you know, such a plan wouldn't work. None of us can make perfect decisions even a majority of the time. And if an investment wealth program required a strict financial diet, it would not only be highly impractical—it probably wouldn't be worth it.

The investment wealth plan described here simply requires that over the course of the next year, you make a handful of clever decisions—perhaps just one or two decisions—and then that you invest the profits from your clever decisions and give them time to grow. That's it.

TWO OBSTACLES TO WEALTH

Accuracy dictates that I inform you there are two obstacles to accumulating substantial wealth using the approach touted in the preceding paragraphs: false affluence and lack of commitment. We should briefly discuss both.

Ironically, one of the major obstacles to actually becoming wealthy for almost everybody is trying to look wealthy. While television series and movies portray the rich as driving expensive cars, living in large homes, and enjoying flamboyant tastes, there's a very basic problem with that image: It's inaccurate. People generally become rich by saving and investing—not by buying everything some advertisement says they should have.

In fact, most of the people who drive an expensive luxury import car—a Mercedes, Jaguar, or Lexus—aren't rich. And most of the people who live in those big homes in affluent neighborhoods aren't rich. They are, to use one writer's description, hyper-consumers. These people spend a lot of money. And they may also have high incomes. But they aren't rich. They lack financial independence. And they often don't really have any financial security. In fact, most millionaires live in middle-class neighborhoods and drive American-made, full-size cars and trucks.

This makes sense, of course. People who spend all of their money buying stuff don't have anything left over to save and invest. And so one of the things that many people need to do—if they are truly serious about achieving wealth—is to make sure that they don't equate false affluence with real wealth. Therefore—and I'm just going to be honest with you here even though it's a bit awkward—you need to make a decision. You need to decide, quite candidly, whether you want look wealthy or be wealthy. I assume that you're reading this book because you want to actually *be* wealthy.

There's also one other potential obstacle on the investment wealth route. Some people lack the commitment. This isn't to say that an investment wealth program requires strict discipline. It doesn't. And I don't want you to think an investment wealth program requires painful sacrifice. It shouldn't. But, well, here's the temptation: In the next few chapters, I'm going to tell you where you can find a bunch of free money in your budget. In Chapter 3, I'm going to talk about how you can make smarter decisions about where you live—and better decisions in this area may provide you with hundreds or even thousands of dollars a year for saving. In Chapter 4, I'm going to tell you how to save money when you borrow. And that should free up another few hundred dollars a year—maybe more. In Chapter 5, I'm going to help you save probably several hundred dollars in the way you buy insurance coverage. And then, in Chapter 6, I'm going to give you additional ideas you can use. After reading a bit, then, you should find yourself with an extra $2,000, $3,000, or $4,000 a year. And at this point, you will come face-to-face with the first temptation: spending this found money on a new car or boat or furniture or some other item. Obviously, if you do that, this plan doesn't work. So you need to make the first commitment: that you will use the savings that the Millionaire Kit helps you find to fund your investment wealth program.

If you resist the first temptation, you will quite quickly come face-to-face with the second temptation: Deciding someday to spend the $20,000 or $50,000 that you've accumulated—and you will accumulate amounts like these very quickly—on a bigger house or to buy a business or to send your son or daughter to some expensive private college. Obviously, you can do whatever you want with the money. It is yours. But to achieve financial independence you need to make a second commitment: that you don't raid your portfolio for some big purchase once you start accumulating a nice chunk of money.

I guess this commitment business sounds kind of funny. But it's really important to consider. Most middle-class people and even many high-income people view their income and their wealth as just money to spend. But you need to think differently. You need to make the commitment that you're going to regularly pump money into your investments and that you're going to let your investments grow. At the risk of being corny, I'd like to suggest that you pause for a moment in reading and consider this commitment. If your reading produces, let's say, $200 of monthly savings, will you commit to using this money for an investment wealth program? When your investment wealth grows to, say, $50,000, will you commit to staying the course? I urge you to do so. If you make the commitment, you will achieve financial independence.

PICKING A WEALTH TARGET

This book's title seems to implicitly suggest that you should pick $1,000,000 as your wealth target. And maybe you want to do that. If it's important to you, a $1,000,000 wealth target is well within reach.

Earlier in this chapter, for example, I talked about three sample cases: a single, twenty-five-year-old ex-smoker; a thirty-something family; and a self-employed fifty-year-old. Each of these sample investors accumulated, rather painlessly I would say, several hundred thousand dollars. However, slightly different—and only incrementally more challenging investment wealth programs—would create million-dollar portfolios for each of these examples.

- Remember the case of the twenty-five-year-old pack-a-day smoker who quits and then saves his cigarette money? If instead of investing his savings into an IRA he uses a typical employer-sponsored 401(k) account, he'll be able to save between $2,600 and $3,600 a year. This amount again varies because the extra tax savings he gets depend on his income. This amount is double the amount he can save in an IRA because of the employer's matching contribution. If this ex-smoker makes the 401(k) contributions over the forty years he'll presumably work and invests in a small-company stock mutual fund (more about this in the next chapter), he will accumulate between roughly $1,200,000 and $1,600,000 in present-day, uninflated dollars by age sixty-five.

• Remember the case of the thirty-something married couple together making $50,000 and saving a truly painless $200 a month through the gambits this book provides? If this couple can instead find $360 a month for savings, which is very realistic, they would probably be able to save about $7,500 a year in their employer's 401(k) plan. The $360 a month grows to $7,500 a year because of employer matching and tax savings. Over thirty years, this couple's 401(k) plan would probably grow to roughly $934,000 in present-day, uninflated dollars if they invest in a small-company stock mutual fund.

• Remember the case of the fifty-year-old self-employed consultant making $100,000 a year and willing to create and then invest a $100,000 financial windfall? If this woman can find a way to reduce her annual spending by $20,000, she could actually contribute about $30,000 annually to a special type of retirement account, called a defined benefit plan, available for self-employed individuals. The $20,000 grows to $30,000 in this case because of the income tax savings. Of course, $20,000 represents an impressive annual savings amount—even when much of this money can come from painless decisions. But note that her ultimate investment balance is even more impressive: She would end up with right around $1,000,000 after fifteen years.

You can see from the preceding examples, therefore, that it is very doable for many people to accumulate $1,000,000. It helps if you start early. And you need to be smart in your investing. But most people—and probably you, too—can get to $1,000,000. However, I want to suggest that you define financial independence as something different than $1,000,000. What I'd like to suggest is this: I think financial independence means you can stop working. All this means is that you need enough investments to produce the money you need to live. This makes sense, right?

It doesn't really make sense to say, "Oh, I want to make a million dollars." It makes much more sense to say, "I want to accumulate enough money, or a big enough investment portfolio, to quit my job."

By restating financial independence in this way, you focus on the amount of investment income you need to achieve financial independence. And when you do this, you can more specifically map out a route for achieving true financial independence.

Insight

Use the **FINANCIAL INDEPENDENCE CALCULATOR** from the companion CD to see how much wealth you need to accumulate to achieve your self-defined state of independence. To do this, follow these steps:

STEP 1   Start the Financial Independence Calculator in the same manner as you start any Windows or Macintosh program.

STEP 2   Enter any amounts you've already saved into the **Current savings** box. For example, if you haven't saved anything yet, enter 0. If you've saved $10,000, enter 10,000.

STEP 3   Enter your current household income into the **Current income** box. For example, if you make $35,000 a year, enter 35,000. Or, if you and your spouse together make $60,000 a year, enter 60,000.

STEP 4   Enter the amount you're currently saving toward financial independence into the **Monthly savings** box. For example, if you're currently saving

$100 each month, enter 100 into the **Monthly savings** box. If you're not saving anything, enter 0.

STEP 5   Enter an estimate of the interest rate you'll earn on your investments into the **Annual interest rate** box. For example, if you think you can earn 5 percent (which is roughly the long-term return of high-quality corporate bonds), enter 5. If you think you can earn 10 percent (which is roughly the long-term return of common stocks), enter 10.

STEP 6   Enter an estimate of the years you'll save and invest into the **Years of savings** box. For example, if you plan to save and invest for the next twenty-five years, enter 25.

STEP 7   Enter an estimate of the annual inflation rate over the years you'll save into the **Anticipated inflation rate** box. For example, if you think we'll experience 3.1 percent inflation (which is roughly the inflation rate over the last seventy years), enter 3.1.

STEP 8   Click the **Estimate** button, and the Financial Independence Calculator estimates the wealth you will accumulate based on your current savings and investing habits. It then estimates the investment income this wealth will produce. Note that both the wealth and income amounts are given in current-day, uninflated dollars.

STEP 9   Optionally, click the **Print** button to print a copy of your calculation results.

Now before we go any further, I want to suggest you take a minute to consider this whole definition of financial independence. Specifically, you need to make sure that your implicit definition of financial independence makes sense by looking at the estimated investment income your investment wealth will produce. For example, if you make the calculations and the Financial Independence Calculator estimates you'll enjoy $26,000 a year of income from your investments, you need to ask yourself whether this is enough. Maybe it is. Maybe it isn't.

You should also compare your financial independence income— remember, this is the amount of investment income your investments will produce—to what you're currently spending. If you're currently making $30,000 but saving $4,000 of this, your current spending equals $26,000. And in this case, you're very reasonable to assume that with $26,000 of financial independence, or investment, income, you can quit working. Remember that this is my definition of financial independence: enough investment wealth that you can quit working if you want because your investments will produce income equal to what you spend.

I don't think it's bad to assume that you'll take a slight drop in your income as you move into financial independence. You might save quite a bit of money by not having certain work expenses, such as clothing, commuting costs, dry cleaning, and so on. Nor is it unreasonable to plan for a little boost in your lifestyle as you move into financial independence because you may want extra for trips, hobbies, and so forth. It is unreasonable and often impractical to plan for a large change in your lifestyle—either up or down—just because you've become financially independent.

Does this make sense? Perhaps an example will help. Let's say you're a single parent making $30,000 a year. In your case, I cannot imagine that there's any good reason to save so much money during your working and parenting years that you can achieve financial independence and live on $45,000 a year. You may feel differently about this, of course. But to my way of thinking, doing something like this requires you to save too large a portion of your $30,000-a-year salary. And, therefore, what you're really saying is, "Yeah, even though I make $30,000 a year, I'm going to live on $24,000 now so I can retire and live on $45,000."

You really do see some people make this mistake of oversaving, by the way: They scrimp and scrape for the forty years they work, living on peanuts. By the time they retire, their penny-pinching is so ingrained, they live the same way in retirement. And then they die with a bunch of money—sometimes millions of dollars—that they never had the good sense to spend. But if you're happy living on $24,000, you should just make that your retirement income goal—and get to financial independence ten or twelve years earlier.

This balance business works the other way, too, especially for people making great gobs of money right now. It is not uncommon to see people living on $150,000 or more a year but in effect planning to retire on $50,000. To me, this makes no sense either: If people really would be happy living on $50,000 in retirement, they should be able to live on less than $150,000 during their working years, which would allow them to save more money and thereby retire with more than $50,000-a-year income.

The bottom line? You need to use your common sense to double-check the reality of the calculations provided by the Financial Independence Calculator. You need to compare your current spending with your estimated financial independence income. To really achieve financial independence, your investment income usually needs to be close to your current income. And it typically doesn't make sense to oversave.

The Financial Independence Calculator, by the way, includes a Balance button that you can click to help you massage your savings plan. If you click the Balance button and your financial independence income is less than 75 percent of your current spending, then the planner increases your monthly saving until your financial independence income equals 75 percent of your current spending. If you click the Balance button and your financial independence income is greater than 125 percent of your current spending, then the planner decreases your monthly saving until your financial independence income equals 125 percent of your current spending. If your financial independence income is greater than 75 percent but less than 125 percent of your current spending, clicking the Balance button has no effect: The calculator assumes your current spending and future income amounts are in balance.

One final comment. Because I can't know the specifics of your situation, don't let me talk you out of following a plan that, according to my comments or the calculator's logic, appears to be out of balance. Maybe there's a really good reason why your plan might be unusual. Maybe you know that you really can retire on an amount that equals 50 percent of your current spending. This might be the case if, at the point you reach financial independence, your children are grown and your mortgage is paid. It's even possible that you might need an amount far greater than your current spending.

What if, in retirement, you want to pay for special care for a disabled child? I'm really only saying that you need to examine with a critical eye any plan that has you saving so much money while you work that you get a big bump in your lifestyle when you reach financial independence. Similarly you need to think carefully about any plan that has you saving so little money during your working years that you suffer a dramatic drop in your living standard when you reach financial independence.

NOTES TO THE DISCOURAGED

Before we wrap up this chapter, let me make a couple more quick comments. Not everybody, but perhaps a significant number of the people reading this, may feel a bit depressed at this point. Maybe it turns out you're inadvertently starting this journey toward financial independence a bit late. Or maybe, through no fault of your own, you've worked through the numbers and things really do seem hopeless. In either of these cases, however, I urge you not to give up just yet.

As promised, in the next chapter I'm going to describe how you can get much and maybe even most of the money that you need for your investment wealth program from other people. Another thing to remember is that if you can begin saving—and I really believe you can rather painlessly find all the money you need—time is your great ally. What this means is that if you're willing to give yourself just a bit more time—even a couple of years—the effects can be surprising. Finally, even if you're starting this journey late, you may be able to accelerate your journey by jump-starting your investment wealth program. As discussed in Chapter 6, you can do so by investing a windfall. And if you don't have a financial windfall handy—who does?—you can often create one.

Another possibility is redefinition of the term "financial independence." As mentioned, this book's implicit definition of financial independence is "sufficient wealth that you don't need to work." That's the logic behind the calculation you made earlier. But if you'd be just as happy working a bit or working off and on—and I think this would actually be true for many people—you don't need as much money. For example, if instead of having to replace all of your working-years' income with investment income, you only have to replace half of it, it's twice as easy to achieve financial independence. And note that this doesn't mean you need to keep your current job. If you love kids, maybe you can help out in a school. If you love dogs, maybe you can get a one-day-a-week job working at a kennel. If you love music, maybe you can teach piano or electric guitar or the saxophone. These may be silly ideas in your case. But you get my point. If you redefine financial independence in a way that says, "For the good of my mind, health, and soul, I want to work a bit," financial independence becomes much easier to achieve.

And then there's one final point I need to make. While it's very difficult to guess what sort of pension plan or Social Security benefits you may have in retirement, and while I don't think you should count on these items, you probably will receive pension or at least Social Security benefits when you retire. Now, nobody gets a lot of money. About the most you can possibly get from the current program in present-day, uninflated dollars is around $1,000 a month, and a married couple who both worked might get at most $2,000 a month. But almost everybody gets at least $300 or $400 a month. And what that means is that in the worst case scenario—let's say you're sixty, have a modest income, and have saved no money to date—you might still be able to run a short investment wealth program like the one described in this book. By working until age sixty-seven or age seventy, you might be able to accumulate an extra $20,000 or

$30,000. This amount doesn't sound like a lot of money compared to some of the figures given earlier in the book. But you could, upon retirement, use this money to purchase a retirement annuity that would produce another $300 to $400 a month of income to supplement your Social Security benefits.

SIX PRINCIPLES OF SIMPLE INVESTING

I f you studied finance in school or have stumbled upon one of the fat investment textbooks, you might think that investing needs to be hell–ishly complex in order to be successful. You might believe, for example, that investing always involves complicated formulas, mysterious cycles, and voluminous quantities of dry information. Fortunately, none of that needs to be true. Investing can be extremely simple as long as you apply six easy-to-fathom principles. So that's what this chapter does. It first describes the six principles. And then it explains how you apply these principles to set up your investment portfolio, which is simply the con–tainer you'll use to create and store your growing wealth.

By the way, at this point in our discussion, it doesn't really matter whether you have any money to invest. In fact, I'm actually assuming you don't. We'll talk about how to remedy any cash shortage a bit in this chap–ter and then a lot more in the chapters that follow. But what I do assume is that you have used the Financial Independence Calculator to come up with a pretty good idea of how much you need to be saving to achieve your objectives. More specifically, you should know how much money you need to put away each month to reach financial independence by some future date. By now, for example, you should know whether you need to be saving $100 a month, $500 a month, or $2,000 a month.

THE FIRST PRINCIPLE:
COMPOUND INTEREST IS THE ENGINE

You need to start your investing by understanding that compound interest is the engine that powers an investment wealth program. You don't need to know how to make the calculations. You can use the software on the companion CD to do that. But what you do want to understand—at least at a gut level—is how powerful compound interest is.

So what is compound interest? I think the best way to explain how compound interest works is by way of example. Let's say that you take $1,000 and invest it in some mutual fund that pays 10 percent annually. If you did do this, you would make $2,500 in interest over twenty-five years. The first year, for example, you would earn 10 percent on the $1,000 and that would equal $100. If you just kept doing this for twenty-five years, you would make $2,500, because 25 times $100 equals $2,500. Okay, so far so good. We haven't actually stumbled on the magic of compound interest yet, but we're close.

Let's take one more step. What happens if rather than spending the $100 of interest you earn a year, you invest it in the same mutual fund and earn another 10 percent? Think about it for a minute. If you take that first $100 of interest you make and reinvest it in the second year, you make another $10 that year. If you leave this $100 of first-year interest invested over the remaining twenty-three years, you'll make another $10 a year of interest for each of those twenty-three years. This interest on interest, or compound interest, will add another $240 to your profits, because an extra $10 a year for twenty-four years equals $240.

And then what happens if you also reinvest the extra $100 you make years two, three, and so on? You also make extra money from this interest on interest. If you work out the numbers, this interest on interest, or compound interest, adds another $3,000 to your investment. So at this point, you've got the initial $1,000 of course. And you've got the $2,500 in interest you earned on the $1,000. And you've got the $3,000 in interest you earned on $2,500 of interest. If you also invest the

$3,000 in interest, you also earn another $2,600. And you can reinvest that.

If you reinvest all the interest you earn, you actually end up with almost $11,000 after twenty-five years.

Do you sense what's happening here? Your $1,000 investment resembles a snowball rolling down a hill. As the snowball rolls down the hill, it picks up snow. Which makes it bigger. So it picks up more snow, which makes it bigger still. The snowball keeps growing as long as it continues rolling down the hill.

The bottom line? If you place money into an investment that earns a healthy rate of return and you reinvest your interest, you sooner or later end up with a tremendous amount of money. In fact, even modest savings programs can produce hundreds of thousands of dollars of wealth.

If the math I've just discussed seems confusing, don't get bogged down with the numbers. Just understand that a regular savings program—assuming that you place the money into an investment that earns a respectable rate of return and that you reinvest the profits—produces significant wealth.

THE SECOND PRINCIPLE: SUPERCHARGE YOUR INVESTING

The next thing you need to understand is that the easiest way to supercharge your investing is by using tax-deductible, tax-deferred investment choices. If you're an employee, your choices might include Individual Retirement Accounts (IRAs), 401(k)s, 403(b)s, and Simple-IRAs; if you're self-employed, they include SEP-IRAs and Keoghs. You might want to review Table 2-1 for a brief description of these investment choices, but the main thing to note is that there are two basic reasons you want to use tax-deductible, tax-deferred investment choices.

The first reason for using a tax-deductible, tax-deferred investment choice stems from the fact that the amounts you save using these investment choices produce tax deductions and, therefore, income tax savings.

Table 2-1

EASY-TO-IMPLEMENT TAX-DEDUCTIBLE, TAX-DEFERRED INVESTMENT CHOICES

CHOICE	TYPICAL MAXIMUM CONTRIBUTION POSSIBLE	DESCRIPTION
401(k)	$10,000	Employees deduct money from their paychecks and then divert the money to an investment account. Often 401(k)s also include matching provisions in which the employer will match some percentage of the employee's contribution.
403(b)	$10,000	Employees deduct money from their paychecks and then divert the money to an investment account. Employers often match employee contributions. [Nonprofit employers use 403(b)s in place of 401(k)s.]
Individual Retirement Account	$2,000 to $4,000	Workers may deduct up to a $2,000 contribution and married workers may deduct up to a $4,000 contribution. Workers covered by a qualified retirement plan can still deduct contributions (or a portion of the contribution) if their income isn't too high.
Simple-IRA	$6,000	Employees deduct up to $6,000 from their paychecks and then divert the money to an investment account. Usually includes employer matching of 2 percent to 3 percent (and at least 1 percent) of employee's contribution.
SEP-IRA and Profit-sharing	$24,000	Self-employed workers divert up to 13.0435 percent of their earnings (with a maximum contribution of $24,000) to a special type of IRA. For example, a self-employed individual making $100,000 a year may contribute $13,043.50.
Paired Plans and Keoghs	$30,000	Self-employed workers divert up to 20 percent of their earnings (with a maximum contribution of $30,000) to an investment account. For example, a self-employed individual making $100,000 a year may contribute $20,000.

For example, let's say, just for the sake of illustration, that you'd like to accumulate $750,000 and to do this, you need to invest $9,000 a year. I've picked these numbers because they make the math a little less messy, by the way. You may plan to save more or less than this amount.

If you can place this money into an investment choice that produces a tax deduction like those listed in Table 2-1, you'll get a significant subsidy. Say, for example, that you pay a 33 percent marginal tax rate on your last $9,000 of earnings. In other words, on the last $9,000 you make you pay $3,000 in federal, state, and local income taxes. This might be the case, for example, if you receive an above-average income and live in a state with income taxes.

In this case, a $9,000 contribution produces a $3,000 tax saving. This means that another way of looking at this $9,000 contribution is that the federal and state government will actually throw in a third of the money: $3,000 of the $9,000 comes from them, and not you. In other words, $3,000, which would otherwise go to paying income taxes, instead goes into your investments. So you don't actually have to come up with the full $9,000, you only need $6,000.

If you work for an employer who provides a tax-deductible investment choice, such as a 401(k) or a Simple-IRA, that matches your contributions, you get another big chunk of money you need from your employer. If your employer provides a 50 percent matching contribution, for example, you only need $4,000 of your own money in order to make a $9,000 contribution. In this case, $4,000 of your money combined with $2,000 in tax savings gives you $6,000 of contribution. With the 50 percent matching, your employer throws another $3,000 into the pot, bringing the total to $9,000.

Now note that how much matching you receive depends on the mechanics of your employer's plan. Your employer may only match 25 percent of your contribution. Or they may match 50 percent of your contribution—but only up to a certain percentage of your income. Or your employer may even provide 100 percent matching.

In any of these cases, however, the basic message remains the same. By taking advantage of tax-deductible investment choices, a huge chunk of the money you need for your wealth accumulation program comes from income tax savings. And if you're lucky enough to work someplace where there's a sweet employer-matched contribution to your savings, most of the money you'll need to fund your wealth accumulation program will come from other people and not from your budget.

Insight

Use the TAX ADVANTAGE ESTIMATOR from the companion CD to see how much "free money" you get by taking advantage of tax-deductible, tax-deferred investment choices. To do this, follow these steps:

STEP 1   Start the Tax Advantage Estimator in the same manner as you start any Windows or Macintosh program.

STEP 2   Enter the monthly savings amount required for your investment wealth program into the **Monthly amount you need to save** box. For example, if you need to save $500 a month, enter 500.

STEP 3   Enter your marginal tax rate—the top tax rate you pay on your last dollars of income, including federal, state, and local income taxes—into the **Your marginal tax rate** box. Most people's top federal tax rates are either 15 percent or 28 percent. Someone who is single pays the 15 percent rate if their taxable income is less than roughly $25,000 and the 28 percent rate if their taxable income is between $25,000 and $62,000. A married couple pays the 15 percent rate if their taxable income is less than about $42,000 and the 28 percent rate if their taxable income is between $42,000 and roughly $102,000. High-income taxpayers may pay higher federal tax rates of 31 percent, 36 percent, or 39.6 percent. If you live someplace where you also pay

Insight (continued)

state or local income taxes, you need to add these tax rates to the federal tax rates.

STEP 4   If you're going to use a 401(k) plan or a Simple-IRA, enter the percentage amount your employer will add to your contribution. For example, if your employer will boost your $100-a-month contribution by kicking in another $50 a month, the matching percentage is 50 percent and you enter 50 (because $50/$100 equals .50, or 50 percent) into the **Employer's matching percentage (if any)** box. Be careful, by the way, that you don't enter the contribution as a percentage of your salary. You want to enter the employer's contribution as a percentage of your contribution.

STEP 5   Enter the annual interest rate you think you'll earn on your investment portfolio into the **Annual interest rate** box. For example, if you think you'll earn 5 percent (which is roughly the long-term return that high-quality corporate bonds have delivered), enter 5. If you think you'll earn 10 percent (which is roughly the long-term return that common stocks have delivered), enter 10.

STEP 6   Enter the annual inflation rate you expect into the **Estimated inflation rate** box. For example, if you think we'll experience roughly 3.1 percent inflation (the average over the past seventy years), enter 3.1. If you want to be a bit more cautious, you might round this number up to 4 percent.

STEP 7   Click the **Estimate** button, and the utility calculates the components of your monthly savings both with and without the use of a tax-advantaged investment. The key comparison is between the savings you contribute out of your after-tax income using a tax-advantaged investment [like a 401(k) or IRA] and the savings you contribute out of your after-tax income if you don't use a tax-advantaged investment. What the calculator shows you—and this is important—is how much of the money you need to save can come from either your employer's matching contributions or from income tax savings. The Tax

Insight (continued)

Advantage Estimator also calculates the effect of income taxes and inflation on your compound interest rate.

STEP 8   Optionally, click the **Print** button to print a copy of your calculation results.

TIP: If you have trouble getting the utility to work, click the **Example** button. When you click **Example,** the calculator estimates your monthly savings if you want to save $300 a month, your marginal tax rate is 33 percent, your employer matches your contributions by 50 percent, the annual interest rate is 10 percent, and the estimated inflation rate is 4 percent.

I mentioned earlier that there's a second reason for using tax-deductible, tax-deferred investment choices. You effectively get a huge boost in the interest rate you're earning by placing the money into an investment choice that doesn't cause your tax bill to go up. For example, if you do pay 33 percent of your last dollars of earnings in income taxes, the income taxes take a big bite out of your interest earnings. A 33 percent marginal tax rate, for example, effectively converts a 9 percent interest rate into a 6 percent interest rate, and it converts a 12 percent interest rate into an 8 percent interest rate. You can test what effect this drop in the interest rate has on your wealth accumulation by using the Financial Independence Calculator.

I cannot emphasize enough the tremendous power of tax-deductible, tax-deferred investment choices. They can easily provide you with scads of free money, and they effectively boost the interest rate your investments earn. In fact, I suggest you consider the availability of tax-advantaged investment choices whenever you think about leaving one job or taking another job. For all practical purposes, tax-advantaged investment choices are essential to a successful wealth accumulation program. Note that the new Roth IRA doesn't allow for tax-deductible investing, only tax-deferred compounding. For this simple reason, you don't want to use a Roth IRA for the investment wealth program that this book touts except in the very special case when you don't have any other tax-deductible investment choices available.

By the way, you may still have tax-deductible, tax-deferred investment choices available to you—even if your employer doesn't provide something like a 401(k), 403(b), or Simple-IRA. If you aren't covered by any qualified retirement plan, tax laws allow you to contribute up to $2,000 a year to an Individual Retirement Account if you're single or up to $4,000 a year if you're married as long as you have earned income equal to or greater than the contribution amount. You can ask your employer about whether there's a qualified retirement plan in effect. If you are covered by a qualified retirement plan, you may still be able to make tax-deductible contributions in 1998 if your income falls under $30,000 if you're single and under $50,000 if you're married, and these amounts rise slightly in later years. For many people, and especially couples, an IRA may be all you need to achieve your wealth accumulation program.

If you're self-employed, you can easily and inexpensively set up your own employer-sponsored retirement plan, such as a SEP-IRA, a Paired Plan, a Keogh, or a Simple-IRA. Any of these plans will give you and any employees tax-deductible, tax-deferred investment choices. For more information, ask any mutual fund management company, including those listed later in the chapter in Table 2-2.

THE THIRD PRINCIPLE: BE AN OWNER, NOT A LOANER

So far, so good. You've perhaps bought into this notion that the investment wealth route is the right way to become wealthy and to make meaningful progress toward financial independence. At this point, you're not sure where you're going to get the $1,000 or the $5,000 a year that you need to fund your wealth accumulation program. But maybe you're starting to agree that if you can somehow find some extra money in the budget someplace, you really could accumulate a tidy little nest egg as long as the interest rates you earn are decent. But therein, my friend, lies a problem. Because, as foreign as this may sound to anyone who reads popular personal finance literature, it isn't as easy to get a 10 percent annual return, or interest rate, as you think. Let me explain.

For all practical purposes, you can categorize your investment choices using two big buckets: ownership investments and loaner-ship investments. Ownership investments give you a percentage, or a slice, of a business or some real estate property, which means that if the thing you own a slice of makes money, you get a slice of profits. The rub is, of course, there's no promise and no guarantee of profits.

Loaner-ship investments mean you've either directly or indirectly loaned some business, government agency, or individual money, which they promise to pay back along with interest. Depending on the trustworthiness of the borrower, loaner-ship investments can be extremely safe and secure. If you loan money to someone who's a flake, of course, loaner-ship investments can also be extremely risky.

At first blush, loaner-ship investments—bonds, debentures, certificates of deposit, government bills, and notes—seem like a really good deal. And over some time periods, such as when the economy gets bad or interest rates fall, loaner-ship investments can be highly profitable.

Unfortunately, over longer periods of time—the sort of time required for the compound interest engine to work its magic—loaner-ship investments typically don't do well enough to work as wealth accumulation tools. Since 1926, for example, long-term corporate bonds have delivered on average just below a 6 percent return (5.7 percent). U.S. Treasury bills, which are essentially high-quality certificates of deposit issued by the federal government, have delivered on average around a 3.7 percent return. Those rates of return don't sound bad, perhaps, but they basically prevent someone from accumulating any real wealth. Once you make the necessary adjustments for inflation, a 5.7 percent return really becomes a 2.6 percent real return and a 3.7 percent return becomes, basically, a 0.6 percent real return. A real return is just one that's been adjusted for inflation.

These low real returns mean that you never get any substantial compound interest and, therefore, that almost all of your wealth comes from the amounts you save. In other words, if you save $1,000 a year for twenty-five years and use loaner-ship investments, you end up with just a little over $25,000 in current-day, uninflated dollars. You might end up with perhaps a little more if you invested in long-term corporate bonds instead of U.S. Treasury bills. And you might end up with a little less if you didn't use a tax-advantaged investment choice for your investing. But in almost any scenario you can imagine, loaner-ship investments don't produce enough compound interest for you to accumulate any real wealth once you adjust for inflation.

 **Insight**

You can easily test the preceding statement using the WEALTH ESTIMATOR from the companion CD. To do this, follow these steps:

STEP 1   Start the Wealth Estimator in the same manner as you start any Windows or Macintosh program.

STEP 2   Enter the current savings amount as 0.

STEP 3   Enter the monthly savings amount as 83.33, which means that over a year you'll save $1,000, into the **Monthly savings** box.

STEP 4   Enter the annual interest rate into the **Annual interest rate** box. For example, enter 5.7 percent to simulate how compound interest might work using long-term corporate bonds or enter 3.7 percent to simulate how compound interest might work using U.S. Treasury bills.

STEP 5   Enter 25 into the **Years you'll save** box to simulate how much compound interest you would earn over twenty-five years.

STEP 6   Check the **Adjust for inflation** box.

Insight (continued)

STEP 7   Enter 3.1 into the **Inflation** box to estimate the future value of your loaner-ship investment after adjusting for 3.1 inflation, which is roughly the historical average of inflation since World War I.

STEP 8   Click the **Estimate** button.

Ownership investments, on the other hand, do deliver the large real returns necessary to work a wealth accumulation program like the one suggested by this book. The long-term return on common stocks since 1926 has been right around 10.5 percent. The long-term return on small-company stocks over the same time period has been a bit higher—about 12.5 percent. The long-term returns on investment-grade real estate probably mirror those of common stocks, although the numbers are a bit more difficult to calculate.

If you simulate how a wealth accumulation program might work with returns like these, you learn that you can actually accumulate a significant amount of wealth. Say, for example, that you were able to come up with $4,000 a year, were able to boost this amount to $9,000 a year through tax savings and employer matching as described earlier, and then that you invested your money over thirty years. In this case, you might very well end up with close to $800,000 in current-day, uninflated dollars if you earned 10 percent a year. And you could end up with just over $1,100,000 in current-day, uninflated dollars if you earned 12 percent a year. So clearly, there's no question about this matter, right? I mean, if you want to take the investment wealth route to financial independence, you have to go with ownership investments. Loaner-ship investments don't work. The returns they deliver just aren't big enough.

Okay, I know what some of you are thinking. You're saying to yourself, "Well, yeah, this is all fine and good, and I'm sure the stock market or real estate or whatever have worked out okay for you. But I'm just a little guy. And I'm concerned about the risks."

I understand your concern, so let me share three comments. First of all—and I'm not going to bore you with the financial theory—the reason you get paid more when you invest in ownership investments, like stocks, is because of the risk. That's the reason you're getting paid more with common stocks than you do with, for example, a U.S. Treasury bill. In fact, financial economists refer to the extra amount you get paid as compared to a U.S. Treasury bill or bond as the risk premium.

I don't know. Maybe that idea doesn't help you. But think about it a bit, because you get paid a big bonus for the risk. What's more, it's this risk bonus that makes the investment wealth route work. That's where the extra money comes from. In essence, you're getting paid more because you're working your money harder.

Now let me tell you something else about the risk of ownership investments. Some people—perhaps you, too—see more risk in ownership investments than there really is because the market bounces about from day to day. You hear that every night on the news. But many days, the day-to-day variations are insignificant as percentages. Yes, the market bounces about a bit. But most of the time, this bouncing about doesn't amount to all that much money.

The day-to-day variability in an investment's value does point out the possibility that an investment you bought for, say, $1,000 may be worth less than $1,000 when you sell it. And that is a valid concern. But it's probably less of a problem than you think. While day-to-day fluctuations in the value of some investment might mean that you would lose money if you held the investment for only a few days, weeks, and even months, the picture changes if you hold the investment for years or decades. In the long run—and by long run, I mean a couple of decades or longer—the stock market really hasn't lost money and almost always beats the stuffing out of loaner-ship investments.

Another way to say this same thing is that while you might very well lose money on an ownership investment over a short period of time because of all the short-term bouncing about, the market tends to bounce up more often than it bounces down. And over time, the greater number of bounces up more than offsets the bounces down.

Let me make one final comment about the investment risks. I know some people—in fact, some very bright people—think that you can't just look at the last fifty or hundred years and extrapolate any trends. How can we know, their logic goes, that in the next fifty or hundred years ownership investments will still prove the best strategy. The world, these people say, is a more dangerous place today than it was in the 1870s or the 1950s.

I can understand it if sometimes you find it easy to slip into this sort of pessimism. But you know what? While maybe some days it does seem that our future is much bleaker than our past, I'm not so sure. If you look back at the twentieth century, we've had two world wars that wreaked unimaginable horror on tens of millions of people, as well as a huge number of minor (minor?), mostly forgotten regional conflicts. In the 1930s, we suffered through a crippling, global economic depression. For most of the last fifty years, we've suffered through a so-called cold war that, to maintain the peace, relied on the thermonuclear threat of mutual assured destruction. And yet, in spite of all these terrible troubles, people have still done best with ownership investments.

Therefore, while I'm not a political scientist or futurist and while I do believe the future is a dangerous place, I also think that it's very logical to assume that prudent ownership investing will still, over the long run, provide the best returns. I'll talk more about how you pick specific ownership investments in the last section of this chapter.

THE FOURTH PRINCIPLE: DIVERSIFY

Here's a fourth principle of investing: You need to hold a diversified portfolio of investment. By diversifying your investments, you greatly reduce the risk that some event—a natural catastrophe, a technological breakthrough, a change in the political winds, or whatever—will reduce or destroy the value of your investment portfolio. Most people intuitively understand this. We've had the motto "Don't put all your eggs into one basket" pounded into our brains. But it's important to understand what financial diversification is. To truly diversify your investments, you need to reduce your exposure to risks unique to a particular business, region, or industry. Let me just give you a couple of examples of undiversified investment portfolios so that you understand what I mean by this.

- If you own twenty rental houses in the town where you live, you're certainly more diversified than if you own a single rental house, but you're not really diversified. Region-specific risks, such as a bad storm or a local rent-control law, might easily reduce or even destroy your investments. And industry-specific risks, such as rising mortgage interest rates or a change in people's housing tastes, might also impair the value of your investments.

- If you own a mutual fund that invests in a particular industry, you're not really diversified either, even if the mutual fund holds hundreds of stocks. For example, a single political development—such as a move to managed health care—might easily reduce the profits and therefore the value of all of the stocks held in a health-care mutual fund. And an exciting new technological development—let's be silly and say it's highly efficient solar energy—might completely change the profits and values of most of the stocks in a utilities mutual fund or a natural resource mutual fund.

The other thing about diversification—and this is just the flip side of the earlier point—is that in order to realistically achieve the average returns that ownership investments are supposed to deliver, you need to have enough investments so that they average out to average. That sounds circular, but I think you probably know what I mean. While the stock market might deliver a 10 percent annual return over the years, some firms will actually go bankrupt and disappear. Others will do phenomenally well and create new billionaires. Everyone would obviously like to pick only the winners. And, sure, that would be best. But the next best thing, assuming that you can't pick the winners, is to just get the average return. And to do this, you need to hold enough different individual investments in your portfolio so their returns average out.

THE FIFTH PRINCIPLE: DOLLAR-COST AVERAGE

The fifth principle is a pretty simple one. As you invest, you want to dollar-cost average. This technique sounds very sophisticated, but it's really not. All it means is that you regularly invest the same dollar amount rather than, for example, purchasing the same number of shares. If you're investing $1,200 a year, for example, you can dollar-cost average by adding $100 a month to your investments regardless of the prices of the mutual fund shares. This means that you keep investing both when the market drops and when the market rises. In fact, because you always invest the same dollar amount, you buy fewer shares of a stock or mutual fund when the prices are higher and you buy more shares when the prices are lower. This makes sense, right? If you're buying mutual fund shares and the mutual fund share price starts off at $10, you can buy ten shares with $100. If the share price goes down $5, you can buy twenty shares. If the share price goes up to $20, you can buy five shares.

The main reason that dollar-cost averaging works, however, is that you continue to invest when the market is both hot and cold. When the market drops next week or next month or next year—and it will—you keep putting money in. In fact, you buy even more shares. And similarly, even when the market gets hot you continue to put money in. Although in that case, you buy fewer shares.

The investment wealth route described and promoted in this book implicitly relies on dollar-cost averaging. In other words, if you're supposed to be throwing $100 a month or $200 a month consistently into your portfolio and you do this, you're using dollar-cost averaging.

THE SIXTH PRINCIPLE: KEEP IT SIMPLE

People who apply the five principles described in the earlier paragraphs of this chapter can hardly help but win in their investing. But I want to throw in one additional principle here, based on my own experiences and observations. Stated most succinctly, you need to keep your investing simple. And there are several reasons for this.

First of all, none of us is a professional investor who can afford to spend more than a few minutes each week thinking about our investments. In fact, such effort is probably counterproductive. If you or I could add 2 percent consistently to our returns, that would be phenomenal and mean we were probably quite a bit more clever than the average professional money manager. Yet this extra return wouldn't actually amount to all that much until late in our wealth accumulation programs. An extra 2 percent on $100,000 amounts to an extra $2,000 a year, for example. And that sounds great. But if the price of that extra return is even an hour a week of time, we're earning less than minimum wage. Most of us would be better rewarded by working a bit more in our regular jobs or even by getting a second job.

Second, any time your investing moves beyond the simple-to-use, easy-to-understand investments described in this book, the decisions become more complex. If it hasn't already happened, you will undoubtedly find yourself presented with all sorts of exotic and often very complicated investment opportunities. Some of the worst in terms of their complexity are whole and universal life insurance policies. But there are many others. Partnership units in real estate limited partnerships are very complicated and can be very risky. Commodities and weird derivatives require a great deal of expertise to manage wisely. And people seem to invent new, highly complex investment products all the time.

Nevertheless, you need to stay away from these products and the people who sell them for two very simple reasons. First of all, any time a product is too complicated for a potential buyer to easily understand, it's very tempting for the person selling the product to bamboozle you, sometimes unintentionally because the product may be too complicated even for them to understand. Second, while you might choose to pay a fee-only personal financial planner, a knowledgeable CPA, or your attorney to help you make the decision, the fees for this service will almost surely eat up any of the extra profits that this supersophisticated, ultra-exotic investment delivers. And this assumes that the complex investment delivers these extra profits, which it may not.

Out of fairness, I should admit that there are investments which do, with some regularity, produce higher rates of return. Good evidence suggests small businesses like the little doughnut shop down the street and entrepreneurial ventures like start-up companies can deliver returns far in excess of the 10 percent or so that the stock market does. Maybe 20 to 25 percent annually. But as a general rule, you can't invest in these opportunities unless you've already got a lot of money or you're a very sophisticated investor with really solid business skills and an advanced degree. It's also incredibly easy to lose your shirt unless you really know what you're doing.

So again, I urge you to stick with simple investments that make perfect sense to you.

PICKING YOUR OWNERSHIP INVESTMENTS

The preceding paragraphs talk a lot about the theory of investing. You now know that compound interest is the engine that powers the investment wealth route promoted by this book. We've talked about the positive effect that tax-deductible, tax-deferred investment options have on your wealth accumulation program. You've heard me make a strong case for ownership investments like stocks and talk up the importance of diversification and dollar-cost averaging. Finally, I've also urged you to keep your investments simple.

What we haven't discussed yet, however, is which specific investment options you should pick. Fortunately, the six principles we've already discussed rather neatly narrow any search. For all practical purposes, you'll need to use a mutual fund. A mutual fund works with tax-advantaged investment choices like 401(k)s and IRAs and makes it easy to use ownership-type investments. Moreover, it allows you to broadly diversify your investment portfolio, use dollar-cost averaging, and effortlessly reinvest your profits, thereby allowing for compound interest. The other thing, of course, is that a mutual fund—or even a couple of them—also lets you keep your financial affairs extremely simple.

As you may know, a mutual fund is just a big pool of money managed by a professional money manager. Individual investors like you and me put money into the fund and then pay this manager and the mutual fund company a small fee calculated as a percentage, which might range from 0.2 percent to more than 2 percent, of the fund's assets to manage the fund.

Which mutual fund or funds should you pick? It actually isn't as hard to make this choice as you might think. If you're an employee presented with a limited set of 401(k) or 403(b) investment choices, you want to pick a fund that invests in a broadly diversified portfolio of ownership investments—like a stock mutual fund that doesn't restrict itself to a particular industry.

If you're self-employed and setting up your own pension fund or you're going to use an individual IRA, you have many more choices. But I actually don't think that should intimidate you. Again, you want to pick a fund that invests in a broadly diversified portfolio of ownership investments.

I am personally very fond of index-style mutual funds, such as Vanguard's Index Total Stock Market mutual fund. With an index fund, you invest in a mutual fund that essentially buys every stock in the stock market. This means, obviously, that you'll never beat the market. In fact, you'll typically slightly trail the market by roughly the amount the fund charges for mutual fund management. For the Total Stock Market mutual fund, for example, this charge equals 0.25 percent. But an index fund means that you know your mutual fund will average out to the average. That maybe sounds defeatist. But roughly 70 percent of the non-index funds—those funds actively managed by professional managers—produce a return less than the market's average.

What's more, with an index-style mutual fund, you don't have to try to figure who the next star fund manager is. Sure, I'm confident that there are a handful of fund managers right now who are just beginning twenty-year runs where they'll produce astonishing returns. But I don't think it's likely that you or I or some magazine editor can identify who they are— even if we spend lots and lots of time looking.

Table 2-2, which follows, lists examples of mutual funds that meet the criteria listed earlier: well-diversified common stock funds. For each fund, I provide the name, telephone number, expense ratio, and the ten-year average annual return if available. You don't need to pick one of these mutual funds, but they give you a good starting point. And you can compare other funds you discover on your own to the mutual funds described there.

You can telephone any of the mutual funds listed and ask for a fund prospectus. A prospectus just describes the mutual fund in enough detail that you can get a good idea of what you're getting into. You'll want to make sure that I haven't made some mistake in describing some key bit of information. And you'll want to make sure that you have enough money to invest in the mutual fund. Most funds have minimum initial investment amounts, although typically these minimums are quite low for IRAs.

As you review the prospectus, you want to pay careful attention to the fees that the mutual fund charges you. You don't want to pay a sales commission, or load, since these can subtract 4 percent to 6 percent from your initial investment, nor do you want to pay 12b-1 fees, which are basically fund marketing and advertising costs. You also want to pick a fund with a low annual expense ratio—which is the ratio of the fund's operating expenses to its value—because the data strongly suggests you get better returns from a fund that charges you less money. Simply put, the fund you do want to invest in should have the following characteristics: It should be a no-load stock mutual fund, it shouldn't charge 12b-1 fees, and its expense ration should be 0.75 percent or lower.

Table 2-2

EXAMPLES OF WELL-DIVERSIFIED COMMON STOCK FUNDS THAT DON'T CHARGE LOADS OR REDEMPTION FEES AND HAVE ANNUAL EXPENSE RATIOS OF 0.75 PERCENT OR LOWER.

FUND NAME	TELEPHONE NUMBER	ANNUAL EXPENSE RATIO	TEN-YEAR AVERAGE ANNUAL RETURN (IF AVAILABLE)
Benham Equity Growth	1-800-331-8331	0.71%	N/A
Benham Income Growth	1-800-331-8331	0.67%	N/A
Dodge & Cox	1-800-621-3979	0.60%	14.30%
Dreyfus	1-800-645-6561	0.74%	9.95%
Evergreen Value	1-800-807-2940	0.65%	N/A
Galaxy II Large Company Index	1-800-628-0414	0.40%	N/A
Lexington Corporate Leaders	1-800-526-0056	0.58%	14.06%
One Group Equity Index	1-800-338-4335	0.33%	N/A
Salomon Brothers Investors	1-800-725-6666	0.69%	11.94%
SEI Index S&P 500	1-800-342-5734	0.46%	13.34%
State Farm Growth	1-309-766-2311	0.13%	13.36%
State Street Exchange	1-800-562-0032	0.62%	13.26%
State Street Research Growth	1-800-882-0052	0.64%	12.66%
State Street Research Investment	1-800-882-0052	0.54%	12.27%
Vanguard Index 500	1-800-662-7447	0.20%	13.54%
Vanguard Index Growth	1-800-662-7447	0.20%	N/A
Vanguard Index Total Stock Market	1-800-662-7447	0.25%	N/A
Vanguard Index Value	1-800-662-7447	0.20%	N/A
Vanguard PrimeCap	1-800-662-7447	0.58%	14.45%
Vanguard Quantitative	1-800-662-7447	0.47%	N/A
Vanguard U.S. Growth	1-800-662-7447	0.44%	12.76%
Vanguard Windsor II	1-800-662-7447	0.39%	13.24%
Vanguard/Morgan Growth	1-800-662-7447	0.48%	12.77%

Chapter

3

THE BIG MONEY IN REAL ESTATE (AND WHERE YOU FIND THAT MONEY)

In the preceding chapters, you've learned and probably verified the notion that an investment wealth program represents your most practical route to wealth. You've also learned that much and perhaps most of the money needed for such a program can come from other sources like the government and, if you're an employee, from your employer. Nevertheless, you still need to come up with a fair chunk of the money yourself. It's very likely, for example, that you'll need to find an extra $100, $200, or $300 a month someplace in your budget. And maybe even more money than that.

This chapter starts your search for this money. It discusses some of the biggest financial decisions you'll make in your life—specifically, those having to do with real estate:

- deciding whether you should buy or rent a home
- choosing a mortgage
- repaying a mortgage early
- refinancing a mortgage
- investing in property
- investing in timeshare properties

What we (you and I, that is) want to do in discussing these issues is find the extra money you need to fund your investment wealth program. But that should be easy. Real estate typically represents a large portion of a person's budget. As a result, there's a very good chance that simply by using your computer to make slightly smarter decisions about, for example, renting a home or refinancing a mortgage, you can find all of the money you need for your investment wealth program.

WHY HOME OWNERSHIP (SOMETIMES) MAKE SENSE

Let's start out with the basics. Fundamentally, home ownership makes sense because it can protect you from inflation. Home ownership offers this protection because by buying a home, you lock in, or freeze, one of your major living expenses: your housing costs.

This makes intuitive sense if you think about it for a minute. If you consider two options—renting a house for $600 a month or buying one with a $1,000-a-month mortgage payment—you know that you're losing money at first by buying a home. Nevertheless, over time, inflation pushes up your rent payment. At the end of the first year, for example, the landlord may raise the rent. And then he may do the same thing at the end of the second and third year. And so it goes.

The cost of owning a home will rise, too, because things like property taxes, homeowners insurance, and maintenance will rise. But the major chunk of your housing expenses—the mortgage principal and interest payment—will stay level.

The end result of home ownership when there's inflation is this: After a while—usually ten or twelve years—it's actually cheaper to live in your own home because of this inflation. And then, at some point, usually far in the future, you pay off the mortgage. At that point, on a month-to-month basis, it's way, way cheaper to live in your own home because what you pay in property taxes and maintenance—remember, you've paid your mortgage—is less than what you would pay to rent a house like yours.

The curious thing about home ownership, however, is this: It often isn't as good an investment as people think. Oh, I know. Your parents made out like bandits. And those friends of yours from college say they've become rich because of real estate. But there are four big problems with home ownership as an investment.

Problem number one is this: While it's true that many people make lots of money in real estate, the sad truth is that they would make much more in some other investment. A few paragraphs ago, I threw out the example of someone choosing between "renting" for $600 a month or "buying" with a $1,000-a-month mortgage payment. Now, maybe a deal like this makes sense. But one thing to consider is where you end up by investing your down payment money and the money you save initially by renting. If you buy a home, you can end up owning a $250,000 house free and clear after thirty years. And that sounds pretty good. But what if instead you invest the money in your 401(k) and end up with $500,000 after thirty years? Clearly, in this example, you haven't really benefited by buying your own home.

The thing to understand, therefore, is that home ownership isn't always a good investment even if it makes money. Sure. Sometimes it is a good investment. But many times it isn't.

 Insight

Use the SUPERCHARGED HOME ECONOMICS CALCULATOR from the companion CD to compare home ownership with another investment. To do this, follow these steps:

STEP 1   Start the Supercharged Home Economics Calculator in the same manner as you start any Windows or Macintosh program.

STEP 2   Enter the rent payment you would make (assuming you rent) into the **Monthly rent payment** box.

Insight (continued)

STEP 3   Enter the interest rate you'll earn on the money you save by renting into the **Interest rate you'll earn** box. If you'll invest in the stock market using a mutual fund and expect to earn the historical stock market return of 10 percent, for example, enter 10.

STEP 4   Enter the annual inflation rate you expect into the **Annual inflation rate** box. If you expect the long-term inflation rate to match its historical average of just over 3 percent, for example, enter 3.

STEP 5   Enter the purchase price you'll pay if you buy a home into the **Purchase price** box.

STEP 6   Enter the down payment you'll make if you purchase into the **Down payment** box. Typically, a down payment ranges from 10 percent to 20 percent of the home's purchase price.

STEP 7   Enter the closing costs you'll pay for the purchase (in dollars) into the **Purchase closing costs in dollars** box. For example, if you'll pay $5,000, enter 5,000. The closing costs you pay as part of purchasing your own house, by the way, will probably include a loan fee, which may run from 1 percent to 2 percent of the mortgage. On a $100,000 mortgage, then, you may pay $1,000 to $2,000 just in loan fees—and possibly even more than this. Note that you will probably also pay several hundred dollars in escrow, title insurance, and other incidental fees. You may also pay 1 percent to 2 percent in state and local real estate transfer taxes. For example, on a $125,000 home, you may pay another $1,250 to $2,500 in these costs. And then, depending on when you close your loan, you may also prepay the interest for the first partial month of your mortgage. By the way, once you apply for a mortgage, the mortgage lender will provide you with an estimate of your closing costs.

STEP 8   Enter the closing costs you'll pay when you sell the home (as a percentage) into the **Selling closing costs as a percent** box. This percentage needs to include the sales commission you'll pay, any real estate transfer taxes you'll pay, the escrow and title insurance costs you'll pay, and any prorated real estate taxes for the current year that haven't yet been paid. The total closing costs for a seller, by the way, can easily run 10 percent to 12 percent.

STEP 9 Enter the annual interest rate you'll pay on the mortgage into the **Mortgage annual interest rate** box. You should be able to get this number from your daily newspaper.

STEP 10 Enter the mortgage term over which you'll repay the mortgage (in years) into the **Mortgage repayment term** (**in years**) box. For example, if you will use a thirty-year mortgage, enter 30. Note that you don't have to enter the mortgage loan amount or the mortgage payment. The calculator computes this information for you.

STEP 11 Enter the monthly amount you'll pay for property taxes, homeowners insurance, and private mortgage insurance into the **Taxes and insurance** box. You can get an estimate of the monthly property taxes expense from a real estate agent or the current homeowner. You can get an estimate of your monthly homeowners and private mortgage insurance expense from the mortgage lender once you apply for a loan. You may also be able to get estimates of these numbers from a real estate agent. If you want to enter an initial guess, you can try entering the monthly property taxes expense as one-twelfth of 1 percent of the home's value. You can also—in the absence of a better number—enter the combined monthly private mortgage and home-owners insurance as one-twelfth of 1 percent of the home's value. For example, if the home you may buy will cost $120,000, 1 percent of this value equals $1,200, and one-twelfth of this value equals $100. You can then use $100 as the monthly property taxes and another $100 as the total combined cost of private mortgage and homeowners insurance.

STEP 12 Enter the monthly amount you'll pay for repairs and maintenance into the **Repairs and maintenance** box. If you move into a new home under warranty, this amount may equal zero your first few years. If you move into an

Insight (continued)

older home, you should probably enter some guess as to this amount—even if the amount is only nominal—say $25 or $50 a month.

STEP 13 Enter your estimate of the number of years you'll own the home into the **Years of home ownership** box.

STEP 14 Click the **Estimate** button, and the utility calculates the information you need to assess a home's investment value:

- the home equity you will "cash out" of the home when you sell it,
- the value of the investment portfolio the renter accumulates by investing his down payment and rent savings, and
- the difference between the two, or the Profit (Loss) of Home ownership value. A positive profit shows you make money by buying a home; a negative number shows you lose money.

STEP 15 Optionally, click the **Print** button to print a copy of your calculation results.

NOTE: The Supercharged Home Economics Calculator ignores the tax benefits of tax-deductible mortgage interest payments and investments in tax-deductible investment accounts like 401(k)s and IRAs. It also ignores the possibility of employer-matching contributions the renter may receive if he invests his savings in a 401(k), Simple-IRA, or similar investment option. For these reasons, the calculator may slightly understate the renter's investment's value.

A second big problem with home ownership, at least when you view home ownership as an investment, is that you borrow money to buy a home. Now, don't misunderstand me. Your ability to get a mortgage is what makes the whole thing work. Few people have enough money to buy a home with cash. But when you borrow money for an investment, you use a trick called financial leverage. Financial leverage means you get most of the money you need for the investment from someone else. If you buy a $100,000 home using a $95,000 mortgage, for example, you're using financial leverage.

Financial leverage isn't necessarily bad. But it has a powerful effect on an investment: It amplifies your profits and your losses. Another way to say this is that financial leverage turns a good investment into a great investment. And it turns a bad investment into a disaster.

But let me give you an example. Suppose you do go out and buy a $100,000 house with a $95,000 mortgage. If you get lucky and your home increases in value by 10 percent, your $5,000 down payment grows into $15,000 of equity. This makes sense, right? If your $100,000 house increases in value to $110,000, you still only owe $95,000 on the mortgage.

Now suppose the home decreases in value by 10 percent. In this scenario, not only do you lose your original $5,000 down payment, but you lose another $5,000 as well. In this case, your home is now worth $90,000, but you still owe $95,000 on the mortgage.

Financial leverage, then, increases your investment risks. Everybody does it. So it doesn't seem like any big deal. But it's important to understand that not only is home ownership maybe not as good a deal as the other investment opportunities you have available, it's also often much riskier. I find it incredibly ironic that people view home ownership as a safer investment than a diversified stock mutual fund.

So now let's look at a third problem with home ownership: It's typically very difficult to convert a home to cash as compared to shares in a mutual fund. Almost always, it takes weeks, months, and in some cases years to convert a real estate investment to cash. And that's bad for the obvious reason: If you need the cash, you may not be able to wait. In comparison, you can typically convert bonds, stocks, and mutual fund shares to cash in a few hours or days. Of course, getting this cash after the actual sale may take a few days. But this is true of selling a home, too.

A fourth and final problem with real estate concerns is transaction costs. Buying and selling real estate is way more expensive than buying and selling other investments. You should typically pay no commission when you buy or sell a mutual fund investment. But for real estate, you'll pay the real estate agent a commission of perhaps 6 percent to 7 percent. You'll probably pay state and maybe local excise taxes of 1 percent to 2 percent. And then there are all the other costs associated with a real estate purchase and sometimes a real estate sale: title insurance, escrow, legal fees, loan fees, private mortgage insurance premiums, and so forth. As crazy as it sounds, these transaction fees can amount to 10 percent or even 12 percent of the purchase or sale price.

Okay, so what do these four problems mean? And what relationship do the problems have to your investment wealth program? I think there are two conclusions you should draw. First of all, make sure you understand that home ownership isn't necessarily a sure winner. Yeah, it can be a good deal even though it's a very risky and a very illiquid investment. But it's very likely that home ownership isn't your best investment opportunity. And that maybe means you should think differently about buying a home. Maybe, for example, you should buy a different type of home. One that's not as big, say. Or, as unorthodox as this may sound, maybe you shouldn't buy a home at all. Maybe you should just rent. Either of these decisions, by the way, would probably produce all the money necessary to run a big investment wealth program. If you decide to rent a $600-a-month apartment rather than buy a condo that requires you to pay an $800-a-month mortgage payment and then another $100 a month in extra expenses, you save around $300 a month. If you decide to buy an efficient, three-bedroom bungalow for $120,000 rather than a big four-bedroom house for $150,000, you'll again save probably $300 a month. Of course, these numbers may be all wrong for your locality, but they give you the basic idea.

There's also a subtler conclusion that you should draw from the preceding discussion and from any modeling you do with the Supercharged Home Economics Calculator. It's almost inconceivable that you'll make money through home ownership *except* when you're buying a home that you'll live in for a long time. Renting a home usually costs less money than owning for years and years. This will be true even when the landlord raises the rent every year.

What's more, you typically need years and years of inflation to pay the transaction costs associated with buying and selling a home. For example, let's say that transaction costs run 10 percent and that inflation runs at an annual rate of 2 percent. In this example, you need five straight years of 2 percent inflation just to pay the 10 percent of transaction costs. And then, even at this point, you still lose money compared to the smart renter because she's invested her down payment and rent savings money.

Neither of these conclusions means that you shouldn't buy a home. But they do mean that most people shouldn't consider home ownership to be an investment. And, perhaps more important, they mean that buying a home needs to be a really long-term decision. If you're going to buy a home, you want it to be something you can live in and with for years and years. An idea like "buying a starter home" that you'll live in for five years rarely works, for example. And an idea like buying a bigger home for your teenage children even though they will soon leave for college may make emotional sense, but certainly not financial sense.

CHOOSING MORTGAGES

If you do decide to buy a home—and most people do—your next decisions concern your mortgage. In general, you've got two important decisions to make. You need to decide whether you want to go with an adjustable-rate mortgage, or ARM, or with a fixed-rate mortgage. And, then, you need to pick the specific ARM or fixed-rate mortgage you want.

Both of these decisions have a huge impact on your finances. And the difference between a good decision and the best decision can easily amount to several thousand dollars: money that can more profitably be used to fund your investment wealth program.

Let's start, therefore, by talking about the first decision you'll need to make: choosing between an ARM and a fixed-rate mortgage. As you may know, adjustable-rate mortgages change the interest rate used to calculate payments every so often—usually every six months. While this is scary, the trade-off is that if you, the borrower, agree to let the interest rate bounce around, the interest rate and especially the starting interest rate is lower. In fact, lenders often set the starting interest rate on an ARM artificially low. But that's the dilemma: an interest rate that jumps around but is probably lower versus a higher but fixed interest rate. Note that there's usually—and should be—an interest rate cap, which is just a maximum interest rate the loan can't exceed.

All that said, what you really need to know is whether an ARM makes more sense than a fixed-rate mortgage given the lower interest rate and in spite of the risk. The key thing with an ARM is whether you can stand to bear the risk of having your payments bounce up. If you've budgeted for a $600-a-month payment and suddenly you're supposed to be making a $700-a-month payment, for example, things can look pretty bleak.

Nevertheless, in general, the risk of having your payment increase isn't as scary as it sounds. Say you're considering two $100,000 mortgage options: a 5.5 percent ARM with a $570-a-month payment and a 7.5 percent fixed-rate mortgage with a $700-a-month payment. If interest rates go up a lot, the ARM borrower might conceivably pay as much as $890 a month roughly two and a half years into the future. This happens if the ARM interest rate rises to 10.5 percent because the interest rate bounces up every six months until the ARM's interest rate reaches the interest rate cap. With the ARM, then, the payment starts off at $130 less a month, but if things go bad, the payment could be roughly $200 more a month. And that's pretty ugly.

But there's actually an interesting opportunity in all this which you should always consider—especially when fixed mortgage interest rates are historically high. If you choose the ARM to get the lower interest rate but make the same payment you have with the fixed-rate mortgage, things look much different. At the very worst, even if interest rates bump up every six months, you're not looking at a $330-a-month increase in your mortgage payment because you've already gotten used to the first $130 a month of increases. This occurs because you've been making the larger

$700-a-month payments that would have gone along with the fixed-rate mortgage.

What's more, by making the larger payments, you more quickly reduce the mortgage loan balance. The extra amount you add to each ARM payment—the first month this equals an extra $130, calculated as $700 minus $570—all goes to principal reduction. Now, this doesn't seem like such a big deal at first glance. But by quickly reducing the mortgage balance right at the very start, you further reduce the size of any future increases.

To summarize then, if you get an ARM but make the payment that you would have made on a fixed-rate mortgage, you get used to a larger payment right from the start. And that's good. What's more, you quickly reduce the mortgage by some extra amount, and that means you reduce the maximum ARM payment by some extra amount. For example, if you reduce the mortgage balance by an extra 2 percent, you reduce the maximum ARM payment by an extra 2 percent. If you reduce the mortgage balance by an extra 5 percent, you reduce the maximum ARM payment by an extra 5 percent. Using the earlier example of a $100,000 mortgage with a maximum ARM payment size of $890, reducing the mortgage by an extra $5,000, or 5 percent, might mean that you reduce the maximum ARM payment by $35 or even $45 a month. So what really happens if you follow the strategy I've outlined here is that your ARM payments fluctuate within a much narrower range of payments—even in a worst case scenario.

In any other scenario, things start to look pretty good. For example, if interest rates don't bump up for a couple of years and then they skyrocket, you don't have to make a large payment on the ARM until the middle of year three. And even when the ARM payment reaches its maximum size, which occurs in year four, your ARM payment growth will have barely exceeded inflation. That's important because if ARM rates are going up because of inflation, you probably also receive cost-of-living adjustments in your salary or wages because of inflation. Or, if you're self-employed, you'll probably be able to increase your prices and therefore your profits because of inflation.

If you get really lucky and interest rates don't bump up for four years, the worst thing that can happen to you is that your ARM payments at some point grow—albeit more slowly than your income probably will because of inflation.

Okay, so what does all of this mean? Simply this: That if you get an ARM but make the same payment you would have made on a fixed-rate mortgage, the worst thing that can happen to you isn't very bad if you're someone who will receive a cost-of-living adjustment. Sure, your payment may grow slightly. But then so should your salary or, if you're self-employed, so might your profits. And you'll be able to cover the extra payment out of your extra income.

What's more—and this is why ARMs are relevant here—if you get an ARM, make the same payment you would have made on a fixed-rate mortgage, and rates don't immediately jump up for a few years, you'll either break even or save money. In the case where you break even because your ARM payment ultimately ends up equaling $700, which is what you would have paid with a fixed-rate mortgage, nothing bad has happened. And you'll actually probably get your mortgage paid off a year or two earlier.

In the case where you save money because your ARM payment ultimately ends up at $100 a month less than what you would have paid on a fixed-rate mortgage, you can use those savings to fund your investment wealth program. Admittedly, it'll be a few years before you begin to see substantial savings. And, of course, you'll want to make sure that you've made enough extra principal payments that your ARM payment won't jump up and cause you headaches should interest rates later skyrocket. But if you're willing to live with a bit of risk and you're disciplined, you can't lose much. And you may gain quite a lot.

Once you've picked the flavor of mortgage you want—adjustable-rate or fixed-rate mortgage—you need to make a second decision. You need to select the best adjustable-rate or the best fixed-rate mortgage available. What you want to do is pick the mortgage with the lowest annual percentage rate, or APR. The annual percentage rate combines all the costs

Insight

Use the ARM ANALYZER from the companion CD to assess whether you can bear the risk of an adjustable-rate mortgage. To do this, follow these steps:

STEP 1 Start the ARM Analyzer in the same manner as you start any Windows or Macintosh program.

STEP 2 Enter your monthly income into the **Your monthly income** box.

STEP 3 Enter the ARM mortgage balance into the **Loan amount** box.

STEP 4 Enter the loan repayment term (in years) into the **Loan repayment term in years** box.

STEP 5 Enter your estimate of the annual cost-of-living, or inflation, adjustments you'll receive into the **Annual inflation in wages** box. For example, if you expect a 3 percent cost-of-living adjustment, enter 3.

STEP 6 Enter the interest rate you would pay if you went with a fixed-rate mortgage into the **Fixed interest rate** box.

STEP 7 Use the **ARM rate** boxes—**Year 1, Year 2, Year 3, Year 4,** and **Year 5**—to describe the worst that can happen with regard to your ARM's interest rate.

STEP 8 Click the **Estimate** button. When you do, the analyzer calculates and then shows the ARM payment the lender will require in the **ARM Pay** column and the no-sweat but growing payment you should make in the **Grow Pay** column. Note that the Grow Pay amount starts out as the fixed mortgage payment but then gets bumped each year by the same percentage as your cost-of-living adjustment. The actual payment you will need to make is just the greater of the required ARM payment or the no-sweat but growing payment shown in the **Safe Pay** column. You want to pay attention to the **Income** and **Safe ARM %** columns. The **Income** column shows how you

Insight (continued)

believe your income will grow over the years it's possible your ARM payment may grow. The **Safe ARM %** column shows what percentage of your income you'll use to make the actual payment, or the greater of the required ARM payment or the no-sweat but growing payment. What you want to do—and this may be obvious—is make sure that the actual payment you'll make doesn't grow to an unmanageable percentage of your income. I personally would be rather nervous if this amount grows to more than a third of your monthly income.

STEP 9   Optionally, click the **Print** button to print a copy of your calculation results.

of a mortgage—the interest charges, the loan fee, any other amounts the lender makes you pay—into one number, a percentage of the mortgage amount. A fixed-rate mortgage with a 7.5 percent APR is in almost every case a better deal than a fixed-rate mortgage with a 7.75 percent APR. So, as a practical matter, what you want to do is pick the ARM or the fixed-rate mortgage with the lowest APR.

I won't spend any more time on this, but please don't underestimate the importance of the cheapest mortgage. Small differences in the interest rate you receive make a dramatic change in the interest you're charged over the life of the loan. A quarter-percent difference on a $100,000 loan, for example, adds an extra $250 a year in interest expenses. Over the thirty-year life of a typical mortgage, that extra amount, stored in a 401(k) plan with 50 percent employer matching, might grow to more than $100,000. So, while I would never suggest you deal with shady or flaky mortgage brokers or companies, it definitely does make good economic sense to talk with several reputable banks and mortgage companies in an attempt to find the best deal.

# Insight

Use the EASY LOAN COMPARER from the companion CD to compare the payments and overall costs of two or three mortgages. To do this, follow these steps:

STEP 1   Start the Easy Loan Comparer in the same manner as you start any Windows or Macintosh program.

STEP 2   Enter the mortgage amount into the **Loan amount** box.

STEP 3   Enter the mortgage term (in years) into the **Loan repayment term in years** box. For example, if you'll repay a mortgage over the next thirty years, enter 30. Or, if you'll repay a mortgage over the next fifteen years, enter 15.

STEP 4   To describe your first loan alternative, enter its annual interest rate into the **Loan #1 Annual interest rate** box and the total loan fees—origination fees, points, and any other costs—into the **Loan #1 Total loan fees** box.

STEP 5   Optionally, to describe your second loan alternative, enter its annual interest rate into the **Loan #2 Annual interest rate** box and the total loan fees into the **Loan #2 Total loan fees** box.

STEP 6   Optionally, to describe your third loan alternative, enter its annual interest rate into the **Loan #3 Annual interest rate** box and the total loan fees into the **Loan #3 Total loan fees** box.

STEP 7   Click the **Estimate** button, and the utility calculates the monthly loan payment and the effective annual interest rate once you roll all the loan fees up with the interest charges. The utility also calculates the total payments you'll make over the life of the loan, and then the total costs, which equal the sum of the total loan fees and the total payments. What you want to do is pick the loan alternative with the lowest effective annual percentage rate, since this produces the lowest total costs.

STEP 8   Optionally, click the **Print** button to print a copy of your calculation results.

REPAYING A MORTGAGE EARLY

One of the ideas that some financial writers like to tout is early mortgage repayment. If you've got a $100,000 mortgage charging 8 percent interest and you make an extra $25-a-month mortgage payment, for example, you save right around $25,000. This sounds like an incredible deal on the face of it. But, except in the situation where you're already making the maximum possible contribution to tax-deductible and tax-deferred investment options like 401(k)s, IRAs, and so forth, early mortgage repayment doesn't actually work all that well. The reasons are that you don't get a tax deduction for your extra principal payments and you don't get to take advantage of the tax deferral. Therefore, if you've been adding a little extra to your mortgage every month to get the balance paid off early, you'll come out way ahead by instead placing the money into an employer-sponsored 401(k) or 403(b) plan or into an IRA.

Let me mention one more thing sort of related to early mortgage repayment. Biweekly or semimonthly mortgage payment plans don't make sense for the same reasons that early mortgage repayment doesn't make sense. You don't get a tax deduction for your extra principal payments. And you don't get to take advantage of the whole tax deferral thing.

Note, too, that the fees some banks and mortgage companies charge for setting up a semimonthly or biweekly mortgage don't make sense at all. Biweekly and semimonthly mortgage payment plans are just another form of early mortgage repayment. You're always better off just adding the fee to the first mortgage payment in the year so it all goes to reduce your principal and then just adding a bit extra to every payment.

But again, don't get sucked into the early mortgage repayment tar pit. It sounds like a good idea. But it's usually not if you haven't already taken full and complete advantage of tax-deductible, tax-deferred investment options like 401(k)s, 403(b)s, IRAs, and so forth.

Insight

Use the EARLY LOAN REPAYMENT CALCULATOR from the companion CD to compare the interest savings of early mortgage payment with your other investment options. To do this, follow these steps:

STEP 1   Start the Early Loan Repayment Calculator in the same manner as you start any Windows or Macintosh program.

STEP 2   Enter the amount you currently owe on a mortgage into the **Current loan balance** box.

STEP 3   Enter the mortgage interest rate into the **Annual interest rate** box. Be sure that you enter the annual interest—which is the rate used to calculate the actual interest charges—and not the annual percentage rate.

STEP 4   Enter the loan principal and interest payment into the **Loan P&I** box. Note that the loan principal and interest amount may be less than the actual check you write to the mortgage company or bank if your payment includes amounts for property taxes or insurance.

STEP 5   Enter the extra principal payment you'll make into the **Extra principal payment** box.

STEP 6   Enter the annual interest rate you expect to earn on an alternative investment in the **Annual interest rate** box.

STEP 7   Enter your marginal income tax rate—the top tax rate you pay on your last dollars of income, including federal, state, and local income taxes—into the **Marginal income tax rate** box. Most middle-class taxpayers, for example, pay top federal tax rates of either 15 percent or 28 percent. High-income taxpayers pay top federal tax rates of 31 percent, 36 percent, or 39.6 percent. State and local income tax rates, if any, need to be added to the federal tax rates.

STEP 8   If applicable, enter the matching percentage that your employer will contribute to your savings into the **Employer matching percent** box.

Insight (continued)

STEP 9   Click the **Estimate** button, and the utility calculates two amounts: the interest you save by repaying your loan early, and the investment profits you accumulate by redirecting extra principal payments into your investment wealth program. (Note that these amounts don't include the principal payments you make.)

STEP 10   Optionally, click the **Print** button to print a copy of your calculation results.

REFINANCING MORTGAGES

Refinancing a mortgage might seem like an obvious tactic for raising the money necessary to fund an investment wealth program. If your current mortgage charges you 9 percent and you can refinance to 7.5 percent, you save interest. If you've borrowed $100,000, the savings equal roughly $1,500 in a single year. Unfortunately, refinancing is trickier than you might at first imagine. In fact, refinancing a mortgage is probably the most complicated financial decision that homeowners have to make. So let me explain.

When you refinance a mortgage, what you really want to do is pay less in interest. Now, to pay less in interest, you *do* want to trade in a high-interest-rate mortgage for a low-interest-rate mortgage. But the interest rate isn't the only thing that affects your interest. Two other variables—in addition to the loan interest rate—determine the interest you pay. Obviously, the actual loan balance is a big variable. If you refinance your mortgage but in doing so take out a larger mortgage, for example, you're not necessarily saving money. A second important—and not so obvious—variable is the loan repayment term. If you swap a 10 percent mortgage for an 8 percent mortgage, that seems like a good deal. But you may not actually save money over the long term if you pay 8 percent on a mortgage for thirty years and you would have only paid 10 percent for twenty years.

Okay, you're probably shaking your head saying, "This makes sense." But people get confused with this stuff all the time. Almost always, they compare only the old mortgage payment with the new mortgage payment. If the new mortgage payment is lower, they assume refinancing makes sense. But that's often not true.

So when does refinancing make good financial sense? And in what situations can refinancing produce savings for an investment wealth program? Well, refinancing makes good financial sense when three requirements are met:

- When the new mortgage balance doesn't exceed the old mortgage balance. You don't want to use refinancing as a way to boost your borrowing. Or at least you don't if you really want to save money.

- When the new mortgage repayment term equals the old mortgage repayment term, because you don't want to use refinancing as a way to stretch out your borrowing. If you do this, you'll really be taking money out of your future budget and putting it into your current budget.

- When—and this is key—the annual percentage rate on the new mortgage, assuming a repayment term equal to the old mortgage, is less than the interest rate on the old mortgage. In other words, you want to make sure that the total costs of borrowing the new mortgage money, which is all encompassed in the APR number, is less than the cost savings of paying off the old mortgage, which include only the interest rate. Please note that you're not comparing interest rates of APRs. You need to compare the APR on the new mortgage with the interest rate on the old mortgage.

Because this APR versus interest rate business can be confusing, let me explain what's going on here. Remember that an APR wraps all the costs of a mortgage into a single, interest-rate-like percentage: the interest charges, the loan fee, the discount points (which amount to prepaid interest), and so on. APRs are wonderful. They let you compare loans when you're shopping for a mortgage. But you need to remember two somewhat tricky aspects of APRs. Here's the first tricky thing to remember: APRs spread the cost of things like the loan fee and the discount points over the life of the new loan—over its repayment term. And that's what they should do. Except that what this means is that if you're refinancing an old mortgage with twenty-five years left using a new thirty-year mortgage, you actually need to pay off the new mortgage over twenty-five years. You need to do this in order to be assured you're saving money, as I mentioned just a paragraph ago. But if you're going to do this—pay the thing off over twenty-five years instead of thirty years—you need to make sure the mortgage company spreads the cost of things like the loan fee over a twenty-five-year repayment term. Yet the mortgage company calculation of the APR may actually spread the cost of things like the loan fee over a thirty-year repayment term. They might do this, for example, because that's the way their computers work or because even though you'll be repaying the loan over twenty-five years the loan is, technically, still a thirty-year mortgage. But anyway, that's the first tricky thing you need to realize.

Here's the second tricky thing: While the APR works wonderfully for comparing new loans, you actually pay all those extra, add-on costs only when you first borrow the money. So once you've paid the costs on the old mortgage, they basically become irrelevant. When you compare the costs of the old mortgage with the costs of the new mortgage, you need to compare the costs you still have left to pay. On the old mortgage, the costs include only the interest charges. On the new mortgage, the costs include the interest changes and all those other fees.

If this business about comparing APRs to interest rates still seems kooky, let me give you a quick example. Let's say you've got a mortgage that requires you to pay $810 a month in interest and that you can refinance with a new mortgage that requires you to pay $800 a month in interest. Looking just at interest charges, it seems to make sense to refinance: The

Insight

Use the MORTGAGE REFINANCING CALCULATOR from the companion CD to determine whether you can truly save money by refinancing your mortgage. To do this, follow these steps:

STEP 1   Start the Mortgage Refinancing Calculator in the same manner as you start any Windows or Macintosh program.

STEP 2   Enter the amount you owe on your current mortgage into the **Current mortgage balance** box.

STEP 3   Enter the existing mortgage's interest rate into the **Current mortgage interest rate** box.

STEP 4   Enter the existing mortgage's principal and interest payment into the **Regular mortgage payment** box.

STEP 5   Enter the new, refinancing mortgage's interest rate into the **New mortgage interest rate** box.

STEP 6   Enter the refinancing costs you will pay into the **Refinancing fees and charges** box.

STEP 7   Click the **Estimate** button. The utility shows your current payment, the new mortgage payment you need to make to repay the mortgage in the same time, and the effective APR on the new mortgage when the refinancing fees are spread over the old mortgage's loan term rather than over the new mortgage's loan term.

STEP 8   Optionally, click the **Print** button to print a copy of your calculation results.

interest rate is lower on the new mortgage, so its interest charges are lower. But let's say that to refinance you'll have to pay $2,000 and that this works out to around $15 a month once you do the complicated math to figure out the monthly allocation. In this case, it doesn't make sense to spend, for example, $15 a month in refinancing costs to save $10 a month in interest. You can see that clearly.

INVESTMENT PROPERTY

Because this chapter describes and discusses real estate, I want to quickly comment on two other topics that'll be of interest to some readers: investment property and timeshares. I'll start with investment property.

While many investors have made large fortunes in real estate, the Millionaire Kit doesn't promote real estate investment. This isn't because real estate can't be a good investment. It can. But it's tricky.

First of all, direct real estate investment—say the type where you go buy some fixer-upper and then rent it out—suffers big disadvantages as compared to the tax-deductible, tax-deferred investment choices encouraged in Chapter 2. If you buy a rental house, for example, you can't deduct the purchase price or the down payment. In comparison, you can deduct amounts you invest using a 401(k) or IRA. As you probably remember from Chapter 2, tax deductibility effortlessly boosts your investment portfolio. And then there's the whole tax-deferral-of-income thing. Amounts you earn from direct real estate investments are taxed.

Another problem with direct real estate investment relates to diversification. Using mutual funds, for example, diversification is easy. Even with only $1,000 to invest, you can widely diversify your investments. But with direct real estate investment, you need hundreds of thousands and maybe millions of dollars in order to achieve the same diversification. Think, for example, about the number of rental properties you'd need to buy in order to have diversification even approaching what you get with a mutual fund owning shares in hundreds of companies and dozens of industries.

And then, of course, direct real estate investment also comes with all the same financial problems as home ownership. Transaction costs are high. Real estate is illiquid. Financial leverage amplifies your gains and losses, which adds to your financial risks.

In short, direct real estate investment really doesn't make sense in most situations. And perhaps most important, direct real estate investments suffer from disadvantages that stocks, mutual funds, and even bonds don't suffer from.

Let me mention quickly just two other things about real estate. First of all, there's a pretty good chance that serious successful investors like you own or plan on purchasing a home. If you own a home, I question whether you need more real estate in your portfolio. If you've got, say, a $100,000 home and a few thousand dollars in mutual funds, do you really need more real estate? If you've got a $250,000 home and a million dollars in mutual funds, do you need more real estate? I don't think you do in either case, but definitely not in the former.

If you're still set on real estate investment, consider a real estate investment trust, or REIT. A REIT is basically a company that owns real estate investments like shopping malls, apartment houses, or real estate mortgages. With a REIT, then, you invest in real estate but you do so indirectly and in a diversified manner.

You can buy shares of REITs in the same manner as you buy shares of stock in companies. Even better, for all the reasons discussed in Chapter 2, you can buy shares of mutual funds that buy shares of REIT. In any event, if you were following this book's investment wealth program, you would buy your REIT shares or REIT mutual fund shares using tax-deductible, tax-advantaged investment vehicles like 401(k)s or IRAs.

The other thing I want to just briefly mention is timeshare ownership. Perhaps I shouldn't include a discussion of timeshares here. I don't know. The thing is, I recently found myself in a room full of people who were considering timeshare vacation property as a way to save money on their vacations. It was pretty clear that timeshare property was anything but a way to save money. Or so I thought. And yet a while later, an acquaintance who happens to be a financial planner told me that he'd taken the bite—that he and his wife had purchased the timeshare interval. So I want to talk about this decision a bit, because this is another area where making the right decision can fund a big portion of your investment wealth program.

Let me start by telling you how developers sell timeshare properties. You walk into a room and the salesperson, after pleasantries, reviews with you the total amount you'll spend on annual vacations over the rest of your life: hotel rooms, airplane tickets, and so on. Then they adjust for inflation and add up the costs.

What you find when they do this—and this is true—is that if you go on vacation every year or every other year, over a lifetime you spend a fortune on vacations. Maybe $100,000. Perhaps $200,000. Or even more. How much you'll spend in total, of course, depends on the sort of vacations you take and on your age. But one recent study suggested the average family spends $3,000 a year on vacations when you add up all the costs: travel, lodging, entertainment, and so on.

Once you agree, "Yes, I will spend a lot on vacation over the next thirty years," the salesperson makes his pitch, which basically amounts to the idea that you'll save money by prepaying your hotel bill. Now they admit that prepaying costs a lot of money. By buying a timeshare, you may spend $10,000 or $20,000 for a week of annual lodging for twenty years or even longer. But, as they point out, you're going to spend the money anyway. And when you compare $10,000 in timeshare costs with the $100,000 you'll spend in vacations over your life, I mean, why not, right?

So do timeshares make sense? Usually not. If you figure out the implicit daily rate you're paying for each night of timeshare lodging and then compare this nightly charge to what you'd pay for an equivalent hotel or condominium room, you usually find timeshares cost you more than just staying in a nice hotel or condominium. (We'll make this comparison in the next Insight box.) So, while the timeshare salesperson may say you can save money—and while he may really believe it—you can spend more money by going the timeshare route.

Note, too, that this "timeshares cost more" business is also true when you buy a timeshare from some individual rather than the timeshare developer. Even though people who resell their timeshare properties often resell the timeshare for as little as half of what they originally paid, these bargain timeshares still often aren't a way to save money.

I don't think, by the way, that all timeshare developers are con artists. Although some of them maybe are. There's a simple reason timeshare properties and timeshare intervals usually cost more money. With a time-share property, you spend vacations in an expensive luxury hotel for the rest of your life. In most cases, you're effectively paying $100 or $200 a night. Sometimes even more. And yet that almost surely doesn't make sense. Even if you do vacation every year, some years you may choose to go camping in the woods, which will cost you a few dollars a night. Some years you may stay with relatives or friends. And still other years, you'll find a 50-percent-off bargain to someplace fun, like Hawaii or the Caribbean. What's more, sometimes you won't mind and may even prefer budget accommodations. I enjoy Paris, for example, but I never stay in a fancy hotel. I enjoy the small, neighborhood hotels for their character—and their price. And the south of France is full of quaint cottages you can rent for $20 or $30 a night.

 **Insight**

Use the TIMESHARE CALCULATOR from the companion CD to determine the implicit nightly room rate for a timeshare property or vacation interval you're considering. To do this, follow these steps:

STEP 1   Start the Timeshare Calculator in the same manner as you start any Windows or Macintosh program.

STEP 2   Enter the total cost of the timeshare property into the **Initial cost of timeshare unit** box.

STEP 3   Enter the annual maintenance fee, usage charge, or membership dues you'll pay into the **Annual maintenance/usage charges** box.

Insight (continued)

STEP 4   Enter the number of nights of lodging your timeshare property provides into the **Nights of lodging you receive** box.

STEP 5   Enter the number of years you'll own or use the timeshare into the **Years you'll own timeshare** box.

STEP 6   Estimate the resale value of the timeshare by entering a percentage into the **Resale value of timeshare (as percent)** box. For example, if you expect to someday sell the timeshare for 50 percent of what you originally paid, enter 50.

STEP 7   If you will use savings to buy the timeshare property, enter the annual interest rate you earn on those savings into the **Annual interest rate** box. If you will borrow money to buy the timeshare, enter the annual interest rate you will pay into the **Annual interest rate** box.

STEP 8   Enter an estimate of inflation over the years you own the timeshare property into the **Expected inflation rate** box.

STEP 9   Click the **Estimate** button, and the utility calculates the implicit nightly lodging charge you're paying by buying the timeshare. The utility also shows the various components of this implicit nightly charge: the annual charges per night of lodging, the depreciation per night of lodging, and the lost interest per night of lodging. But what you have to do is compare the implicitly nightly lodging charge with what you might pay if you didn't own the timeshare property.

STEP 10   Optionally, click the **Print** button to print a copy of your calculation results.

Chapter

4

BORROWING TIME

I'm not going to beat around the bush with you. The ways that you borrow money will greatly affect your investment wealth program. If you're smart about the way you borrow, for example, you'll find it easy to accumulate wealth. If you maybe haven't been so smart, you'll find it very difficult to begin accumulating wealth. For these reasons, this chapter talks about how you should and shouldn't borrow money.

But let me say one other quick thing before we start: If you are someone who's gotten in over your head with debt—and many people fall into this category—don't get annoyed or discouraged by what you read here. The real purpose of this chapter is to help you organize your debts in a way that means you have money for your investment wealth program. And if you are in "over your head," just straightening out your debts will provide all the money you need.

USING A CREDIT CARD

Let's start by talking about credit cards. The way that you use your credit cards has a huge impact on your financial affairs—probably much larger than you realize. And, more important, the way that you use a credit card is easy to change. It's very possible that by just "getting smart" about your credit cards, for example, you can find all the money you need for an investment wealth program.

The first thing we should talk about is whether you should even use a credit card. While you might be tempted to just skip over this point, let me tell you that studies show you and I spend more when we shop with a credit card. One study, for example, says 23 percent more.

I'm not sure about the exact percentages. But my intuition tells me the gist of this research is true. If you spend cash or write a check, the amount of money you have in your pocket or in your checking account will sometimes and maybe often limit your purchases. If you buy lunch with a credit card at some deli, for instance, you may not even think about the price of a $5 sandwich. On the other hand, if you've only got a pocketful of change, you may choose the 60¢ bagel. Okay, maybe these numbers are all wrong for you. Maybe you would never spend $5 on a sandwich. And maybe a 60¢ bagel would never be enough for lunch. But you see the point. If you're spending cash or writing a check, you will sometimes select a less expensive substitute. Maybe you won't buy that jazz CD, a second magazine, or the more expensive T-shirt. And, if you are just slightly more economical in your purchases, the savings quickly add up. A buck here and a buck there—pretty soon you've got all the money you need to run an investment wealth program. So that's the first thing you should realize when using a credit card: Just by using a card, you probably spend more.

A second thing you should recognize is that the extra cost of using a credit card—that extra money you spend—never pays for the benefits of an affinity or cash-back card. A 2 percent cash-back program doesn't come close to paying for the extra expense of using a credit card if you're always charging 20 percent or 25 percent more with the credit card. A 5 percent rebate on a new car doesn't come close, for example, and we don't even have to consider the point that you may end up with a car that you don't need or like. And then a free airplane ticket for spending $25,000, as might be the case on an airline card, also doesn't really save you money. Free airplane tickets often work out to roughly 1 percent or 2 percent discounts, by the way.

Please note, too, that everything I've said so far is true even if you pay off your credit card balance in full each month and therefore never pay any finance charges. You still spend more by using a credit card. If you spend a couple of hundred dollars a month on your credit card, for example, you may be overspending by about $50 a month. And that $50 might be everything you need to run your investment wealth program.

Insight

Use the **COST OF HABIT CALCULATOR** from the companion CD to explore how *not* using a credit card might add to your wealth. To do so, follow these steps:

STEP 1   Start the Cost of Habit Calculator in the same manner as you start any Windows or Macintosh program.

STEP 2   Enter 20 percent of the amount you regularly charge on your credit card into the **I regularly spend this amount** box. Note: The implicit assumption is that if you didn't use a credit card—and you believe the studies—you'll probably spend 20 percent less. To calculate 20 percent of the amount you regularly spend, you can multiply your average charges by 0.2.

STEP 3   Mark the monthly button in the **I spend this amount every** set of option buttons.

STEP 4   Enter an estimate of the interest rate you'll earn on your investments into the **Annual interest rate** box. For example, if you think you'll earn 8 percent, enter 8.

STEP 5   Enter an estimate of the years you'll save and invest into the **Years of investing** box. For example, to see how much you might accumulate over twenty-five years by not using a credit card, enter 25.

Insight (continued)

STEP 6 Enter an estimate of your marginal income tax rate—the top tax rate you pay, including federal, state, and local taxes—into the **Marginal income tax rate** box. Most middle-class taxpayers, for example, pay top federal tax rates of either 15 percent or 28 percent. High-income taxpayers pay top federal tax rates of 31 percent, 36 percent, or 39.6 percent. State and local tax rates need to be added to the federal tax rates.

STEP 7 If you're an employee and your employer matches your contributions to a Simple-IRA or 401(k), enter the matching percentage your employer will contribute to your savings into the **Employer's matching percentage** box. For example, if you can contribute your credit card savings to an employer-sponsored 401(k) plan with 50 percent matching, enter 50.

STEP 8 Use the **Tax-deductible** option buttons—**Yes** and **No**—to indicate whether you can invest additional money using a tax-deductible investment choice, such as an IRA or a 401(k).

STEP 9 Use the **Tax-deferred** option buttons—**Yes** and **No**—to indicate whether your employer will match your investments.

STEP 10 Click the **Estimate** button, and the Cost of Habit Calculator estimates the wealth you accumulate because you stop using a credit card, thereby saving money, and then invest the money.

STEP 11 Optionally, click the **Print** button to print a permanent copy of your calculation results.

If you carry a credit card balance, of course, things get even uglier because the interest rates are so high on credit cards. In the case where you carry a balance of a couple of thousand dollars and then charge a couple hundred dollars a month on your credit card, you might also be paying close to $50 a month in interest charges. So—and this is the great surprise for some people—just using a credit card in a relatively modest way may be taking around $100 a month out of your budget. In other words, you may spend an extra $50 a month just because you're using the credit card and then you may spend another $50 a month on finance charges. I can guess there are a bunch of ways you'd rather spend the $100, of course. But I'd like you to use the $100 to become wealthy. If you want to explore the effect of saving money and not paying finance charges, you can also use the Cost of Habit Calculator, as described in the preceding Insight box. The only thing you need to do differently is add your monthly finance charges to the amount you entered in step 2.

But let's move on. Let's say that you do need to use a credit card per-haps for convenience reasons or because of your work or because you are already carrying a balance. What should you do?

Actually, once you do decide to use or find yourself of necessity using a credit card, it's pretty easy to pick a card. If you don't carry a balance, pick a card that doesn't charge you any fee. To minimize fees, you also don't want to have more than a card or two. If you're not carrying a bal-ance, the interest rate is irrelevant because you'll never pay finance charges. What you want is a free or low-fee card.

If you do carry a balance, pick the credit card or find a credit card with a lower interest rate. Practically speaking, it doesn't matter what the fee is in this case because the finance charges grossly outweigh the annual fee. Remember that even on a relatively modest $1,000 credit card balance, you may be paying close to $200 a year in finance charges.

But please, please, please: Attempt to break the credit card habit if you're looking for money to fund an investment wealth program. Using a credit card and carrying a credit card balance are so expensive that chang-ing just this one habit often provides all the money you need to reach financial independence.

A bit later in the chapter, in the section entitled Getting Out of Debt, I'll describe some tricks and techniques that you can use to get out of debt, including how you get out of credit card debt. Before we jump into that discussion, however, I want to talk with you about how you make the best choices concerning the other types of borrowing you'll do. Once you have that background information, you can look at all of your debts together and figure out the very smartest way to unburden yourself.

PICKING A LOAN

Okay, on to another debt management topic: picking a loan. To some people's surprise, picking a loan actually isn't very difficult. Two rather simple rules apply. The first rule is that you want to repay the loan by the time the item you're borrowing money for wears out. If you borrow money to buy a car, for example, you want to repay the car loan by the time you need a new car. If you borrow money to buy a house, you want to make sure that the mortgage is or can be repaid by the time the house wears out.

This rule makes sense, right? You don't want to still be paying off some old loan for an item that's long since worn out. When the item has worn out, you want a replacement. And if you need to borrow money for the replacement and at the same time are still repaying the old loan, well, plainly, such an arrangement doesn't work.

This first rule explains why it doesn't make sense to borrow money for trips, food, clothing, and anything else you consume, or use up, almost immediately. By the next time you want to go on a trip, eat, or get a new shirt, you'll likely still be paying off your original loan. If you then need a second loan for the new consumable, you've suddenly got two loans or a larger credit card balance. And this situation quickly gets worse and worse until it's unbearable. Enough said about the first rule of borrowing money.

The second rule of borrowing money is the one that's obvious although not always easy to apply: You want to pick the loan with the cheapest cost. To do that, you pick the loan with the lowest annual percentage rate, or APR. The APR combines all the costs of a loan—interest, fees, add-on costs, and so forth—into one number: a percentage of the loan balance. By picking a loan with the lowest interest rate, you are almost assured of getting the best deal possible. And please note that seemingly small differences in an APR can add up to big dollars—especially over the life of a long-tern loan (such as a mortgage).

 Insight

Use the **EASY LOAN COMPARER** from the companion CD to compare the payments and overall costs of two or three loans. To do this, follow these steps:

STEP 1   Start the Easy Loan Comparer in the same manner as you start any Windows or Macintosh program.

STEP 2   Enter the amount you want to borrow into the **Loan amount** box.

STEP 3   Enter the repayment term (in years) into the **Loan repayment term in years** box. For example, if you'll repay a car loan over the next five years, enter 5.

STEP 4   To describe your first loan alternative, enter its annual interest rate into the **Loan #1 Annual interest rate** box and the total loan fees—origination fees, points, and any other costs—into the **Loan #1 Total loan fees** box.

STEP 5   Optionally, to describe your second loan alternative, enter its annual interest rate into the **Loan #2 Annual interest rate** box and the total loan fees into the **Loan #2 Total loan fees** box.

STEP 6   Optionally, to describe your third loan alternative, enter its annual interest rate into the **Loan #3 Annual interest rate** box and the total loan fees into the **Loan #3 Total loan fees** box.

STEP 7   Click the **Estimate** button, and the utility calculates the monthly loan payment, the effective annual interest rate, the total payments you'll make over the life of the loan, and then the total costs. The effective interest

Insight (continued)

rate combines the loan fees with the interest charges, so it really works like an APR. The total costs equal the sum of the total loan fees and the total payments. What you want to do is pick the loan alternative with the lowest effective annual percentage rate, since this produces the lowest total costs.

STEP 8   Optionally, click the **Print** button to print a copy of your calculation results.

One thing I should mention about comparing loans, however, is that when a lender calculates the APR on a loan, he assumes that you'll repay the loan over the specified term. If you're borrowing money using a five-year car loan, for example, the lender assumes that you'll repay the loan over five years and not earlier. Usually, the lender's assumption is correct. But realize that in calculating the APR, the lender spreads out the non-interest charges over the repayment term, too. The APR calculation on a five-year car loan, for example, might assume you will pay interest charges plus another, say, $10 a month. Now here's the problem: If you pay off the loan sooner than the lender expects, you need to pay all the noninterest charges off over a shorter period of time. And in this case, it may be that the APR calculation needs to assume that you're really paying $20 a month in these noninterest charges rather than merely $10 a month. Therefore, if there are noninterest charges associated with a loan and if you do repay the loan early, the APR goes up. The loan document might say the APR is 10 percent, for example, but that's the case when the loan is repaid over five years. If you repay the loan early over, say, two years, it might be that the APR is really 12 percent.

What do you do about this potential problem? Well, if you're not going to repay loans early, you don't need to worry about it. You can also get loans with repayment terms that match your plans. By doing this, the lender calculates the APR assuming the appropriate repayment term.

Finally, you can use the Easy Loan Comparer utility to estimate the effective APR. The preceding Insight box describes how you use this program.

USING HOME EQUITY LOANS

Ah, yes. Home equity loans. If you own your home, you've gotten the advertisements from banks and finance companies. What they suggest you do is borrow money for something—perhaps a new car—but secure the loan using the equity in a home you own.

The attraction of a home equity loan is twofold: Rather than borrow money through a high-interest-rate loan or credit card, you instead borrow money through a lower-interest-rate home equity loan. And then, in addition to the whole "high-interest-rate versus low-interest-rate" thing, the advertisements also always tell you to consult your tax advisor because home equity loans may be tax deductible because, in general, the interest on home equity loans of less than $100,000 is tax deductible if you itemize.

On the face of it, home equity loans can make sense. A home equity loan allows you to swap low-cost, tax-deductible home equity loan debt costing perhaps 10 percent annually for high-cost, consumer credit debt costing 18 percent or 20 percent annually. Let's say you've got $10,000 of credit card debt costing you 20 percent, or $2,000 a year. If you go get a $10,000 home equity loan costing you 10 percent, or $1,000 a year, you save about $1,000 a year in interest. If you itemize your tax deductions, you'll also get a tax deduction, which will probably be worth roughly another $300 to $400 depending on your income and the state you live in. And what these savings mean is that if you do swap the $10,000 of credit card debt for a $10,000 home equity loan and you use all the savings for debt repayment, you can painlessly become free of credit card debt in a little over five years. The business about painlessly getting out of debt is the important part, by the way. With a home equity loan, you don't make extra sacrifices. You use the interest rate savings and the tax savings to get you out of debt.

And then once you pay off the home equity loan, you could use the extra money you should now have for your investment wealth program. At the point you had repaid the home equity loan, you probably have around $2,000 a year in savings that, over thirty years, could grow to almost $230,000 of wealth if you invest the savings into an IRA and to almost $340,000 if you invest the savings into a 401(k) plan or Simple-IRA that provides employer matching.

Now let me stop for a minute and respond to what I'm guessing is your first impression regarding this whole notion. I guess that you're thinking thirty years—the number used in this example—is a long time. You're right. It is. But if you're thinking this way, I respectfully suggest that you're missing the point. In a very reasonable scenario, what's happening is that by swapping a home equity loan for credit card debt and then showing a bit of discipline, you get several hundred thousand dollars of extra wealth. There's no pain involved. Just a bit of paperwork. And, of course, some personal discipline.

So, clearly, home equity loans can be marvelous tools.

However, to be quite frank, I get nervous when people apply the tactic just described. Sure. I'll agree that it does make sense to choose debts with lower interest rates. That's obvious. And if the loan amounts involved are large, saving 10 percent or 12 percent annually can easily produce big interest savings.

Unfortunately, for some people, there can be two big problems with home equity loans. The first problem is that while it's okay to substitute a home equity loan in place of a consumer credit loan like a car loan or a credit card balance, some people don't actually substitute. They instead use the home equity loan to increase their borrowing. For example, someone may choose to use a home equity loan to pay off all of their credit card balances and maybe a car loan, too. And while that might make sense, if this person then goes out a few months later and begins charging purchases on the credit cards again, they aren't really saving money. All they've really done is use a home equity loan to increase their borrowing. For this reason, if you're someone who finds it easy to borrow money using consumer credit loans or credit cards, you need to think long and hard before using a home equity loan.

There's a second problem with home equity loans, too: Because home equity loans are secured by your home and a home will last for decades or longer, the bank happily sets the repayment term for a home equity loan for a long time. A ten-year repayment term is very common, for example. Okay, that sounds great. And it makes for nice, low payments. But it typically violates the first rule of borrowing—the one that says you need to repay a loan by the time the item you're borrowing to buy is worn out.

You can go out, for example, and use a ten-year home equity loan to buy a new car. But if the car wears our after, say, seven years, you'll still have three years of payments left on what's essentially your car loan. If you then need to again borrow money to buy a replacement vehicle, you'll now be making payments both for the car you no longer own and the new car you've just purchased. And that just doesn't work. Eventually— and probably not all that far into the future—you come to a day of reckoning where you don't have any good choices—only a whole bunch of bad ones. For example, "Should I not buy a new car even though my old car is worn out?" and "Should we sell our home so we can afford the cars or clothes we've already bought?"

To make sure that you don't get into home equity loan trouble of this sort, you'll want to follow several rules of thumb. If you will use a home equity loan to pay off a credit card balance, follow these rules:

- Compare the credit card interest rate with the home equity loan interest rate and verify that you're truly getting significant interest rate savings. You should save at least 5 percent—and hopefully a lot more.

- Use the home equity loan to reduce, not increase, your credit card borrowing. In other words, use your home equity loan proceeds to immediately pay down your credit card balance. Don't just spend the money.

• Direct all of your interest rate and tax savings toward quickly repaying the home equity loan and then, after that, funnel all savings into your investment wealth program.

If you will use a home equity loan to pay off a car loan, the same basic rules as just described apply. In addition, you should make sure that you have the home equity loan repaid by the time, and preferably long before, whatever you're borrowing to buy wears out. If you're buying a new car and you figure it'll last eight or ten years, for example, get the home equity loan paid off in five years.

Insight

Use the HOME EQUITY LOAN ANALYZER from the companion CD to estimate the interest savings you might enjoy by using a home equity loan to consolidate consumer credit debts (like credit cards and car loans). To do this, follow these steps:

STEP 1   Start the Home Equity Loan Analyzer in the same manner as you start any Windows or Macintosh program.

STEP 2   Enter the amount you want to borrow into the **Total consumer credit debts** box.

STEP 3   Enter the average annual interest rate your credit cards or consumer loans charge into the **Consumer credit interest rate** box. For example, if you want to use a home equity loan to repay a car loan charging 12 percent interest, enter 12.

STEP 4   Enter the annual interest rate your home equity loan will charge into the **Home equity loan interest rate** box.

STEP 5   Enter your marginal tax—the top tax rate you pay on your last dollars of income, including federal, state, and local income taxes—into the **Your marginal tax rate** box.

Insight (continued)

STEP 6   Click the **Estimate** button, and the utility calculates the several pieces of data that you'll find useful both for assessing the financial effect of a home equity loan and for planning repayment. For example, the **Effective interest rate "drop"** shows whether you'll actually pay a lower interest rate on a home equity loan. Usually you do, but you need to check this. And then the **Approximate first-month tax savings** shows how much interest you save the first month of the home equity loan. The calculator suggests a monthly home equity loan payment by adding the monthly interest you used to pay to the tax savings you'll get by using a home equity loan. This is the **Suggested home equity payment** amount. Finally, the **Years to repay using suggested home equity loan payment** shows how long it will take to repay the loan using the suggested payment. You want to make sure this repayment term doesn't violate the first rule of borrowing discussed earlier.

STEP 7   Optionally, click the **Print** button to print a copy of your calculation results.

GETTING OUT OF DEBT

If you get in over your head with debt, it's natural to want to get out of debt. And it's probably not a bad idea. The extra cost of using a credit card and carrying even relatively modest credit card balances can equal the money needed for an investment wealth program.

Unfortunately, there are no magic tricks for getting out of debt. Some of the things I've already mentioned—like not using credit cards or using a home equity loan for consolidation—will help. But in the end, you just need to begin spending less than you earn. Any leftover money then needs to go to paying down your debts.

In paying down your debts, start with your most expensive debts. These debts will probably be your credit cards. Then, when you get the most expensive debt paid, start paying down the next most expensive. Continue this process until you've paid down your debts to a manageable and prudent level. As noted before, that probably means when you've paid off all of your credit card balances and that you'll be able to pay off any of your remaining loans by the time the item you borrowed to buy wears out.

Let me mention one more thing about getting out of debt. As long as you're not in over your head—and I'd agree with the basic lender's rule that says you shouldn't have debt payments greater than one-third of your income—you shouldn't postpone starting an investment wealth program until you get out of debt. Sure, getting out of debt is great. And if you pay off your car loan or even your mortgage early, you'll probably never regret it. But as noted in Chapter 1, time is of the essence in your investment wealth program. You want to begin contributing money to your investment portfolio as soon as possible. You want to begin getting tax deductions and possible employer matching contributions so you can boost your savings as soon as possible. You want to begin earning tax-deferred investment income so you can start the compound interest engine working as soon as possible. You'll get a far bigger bang for your buck by using tax-deductible, tax-deferred investment choices than you will by paying off, for example, your mortgage early.

Therefore, once you've got any expensive personal loans and your credit card balances paid down, go ahead and start your investment wealth program. And do make sure that you don't violate the first rule of borrowing.

LEASING A CAR

People sometimes ask me whether leasing a car is a good deal, so let me just quickly address this question. While as a practical matter, leasing really amounts to a long-term rental, not a purchase—and this explains the lower monthly payments and the absence of a down payment—in general, you want to view leasing as just another way to finance a car purchase. With a car loan, you make a down payment and then you pay off a loan. With a lease, you make the lease payments and then you pay off or can pay off the residual, which is sort of like a back-end down payment.

To compare leasing with borrowing, what you want to do is look at the implicit APR charged by the lease and compare this percentage to the APR charged by a bank or finance company. If the lease's APR is lower than the bank loan's APR, leasing costs you less money.

 **Insight**

Use the SMART LEASE CALCULATOR from the companion CD to estimate the implicit interest rate you pay by leasing a vehicle. To do this, follow these steps:

STEP 1 Start the Smart Lease Calculator in the same manner as you start any Windows or Macintosh program.

STEP 2 Enter the purchase price of the vehicle you may lease into the **Purchase price of car** box.

STEP 3 Enter any nonrefundable costs or fees you'll pay at the start of the lease into the **Upfront leasing costs** box.

STEP 4 Enter any refundable security deposit you'll make at the start of the lease into the **Security deposit** box.

STEP 5 Enter the monthly lease payment you'll make into the **Monthly lease payment** box.

STEP 6 Enter the number of regular monthly lease payments you'll make into the **Number of lease payments** box.

STEP 7 Use the **Payments made at** buttons—**Beginning of month** and **End of month**—to indicate when your lease payments must be made. Usually lease

Insight (continued)

payments are made at the start of the month, unlike loan payments, which are made at the end of the month.

STEP 8   Enter the price for which you'll be able to purchase the car into the **Residual** box.

STEP 9   Click the **Estimate** button, and the utility calculates the implicit interest rate you'll pay if you lease the car. To determine whether leasing makes financial sense, you can compare this implicit interest rate to the interest rate you would pay on a regular car loan.

STEP 10   Optionally, click the **Print** button to print a copy of your calculation results.

BORROWING TO INVEST

Before we wrap up this discussion of borrowing, we should talk a bit about financial leverage. As you may know, financial leverage means you borrow money and then invest it. For example, if you buy a rental property using a mortgage, you're using financial leverage. And if you borrow money for an IRA contribution, you're using financial leverage.

Financial leverage works, as noted in the previous chapter, when the interest rate you earn on your investment exceeds the interest rate you pay to borrow the money. For example, if you borrow money at 7 percent and then you invest in the stock market and earn 10 percent, your profits not only pay all your borrowing costs, they also deliver an extra 3 percent profit—even though you haven't really invested any of your own money.

Financial leverage is often popular with personal finance writers because it amplifies your profits. Say, for example, that you have $1,000 to invest in the stock market and that the market earns 10 percent. In this situation, you earn $100 in profit. If you borrow another $9,000 and pay

8 percent interest, you can invest $10,000 in the stock market, thereby earning $1,000 in interest. If from this $1,000 in profits, you pay $720 in interest expense (calculated as 8 percent of $9,000), your net profits equal $280. By using financial leverage you earn $280 instead of $100. You almost triple your profits.

Leverage works great in concept because with very little money you can make almost vulgar amounts of money. In the scenario we've just discussed, for example, instead of making a 10 percent return on your investment (calculated as $100/$1,000), you would make a 28 percent return on your investment. When you start compounding your interest using high rates of return like 28 percent, an investment portfolio quickly grows into a huge treasure. If you earn 10 percent on an IRA into which you place $2,000 a year, for example, you get just over a quarter of a million dollars after thirty-five years and after adjusting for inflation. If you instead earn 28 percent, you get just under $20,000,000. You read right: almost twenty million.

Despite the fact that financial leverage seems more like financial nirvana than anything else, I don't think it makes sense as an element in an investment wealth program. And there are a couple of reasons for this. First of all, financial leverage not only amplifies your profits, it also amplifies any losses. So with leverage you're bearing considerably more risk. That risk may seem like it's worth it. I mean, hey, you know: $20,000,000 is a lot of money. But I'm not sure it is. Does it really make sense to give up almost sure, millionaire-class riches for a possible king's ransom? It's your call, of course. But I don't think it does.

There's also a second, more practical problem with leverage. Stated most simply, it's not really sustainable. In the case where you're borrowing money to boost your return from 10 percent to 28 percent, for example, you're borrowing nine out of every ten dollars from someone else. And while that might be possible on a limited basis or over a short period of time, you wouldn't be able to do so indefinitely. Going back to the $20,000,000 IRA account, for example, this borrowing would actually mean you'd borrowed roughly $180,000,000 million by the time your account had grown to be worth $20,000,000. That would not only be impractical—it would also be impossible.

All of this maybe sounds like gobbledygook, I know. But do take away two important thoughts. First, while financial leverage amplifies your profits, it also amplifies your losses—and that dramatically and unnecessarily increases your risks. Second, financial leverage typically isn't sustainable (at least in the context of an investment wealth program) on a long-term basis.

FINANCIAL SAFETY NETS

There's a saying among circus performers that while there are bold high-wire acrobats and there are old high-wire acrobats, there are no bold, old high-wire acrobats. And the truth of this statement explains why high-wire acrobats use safety nets. Sometimes, even if you're good and careful and generally lucky, you fall. And if you do fall, you want to make sure that there is a safety net waiting to catch you.

This business about safety nets applies with equal force to your personal finances and any investment wealth program for two reasons. First and foremost, you don't want some little foul-up or spat of bad luck to stop your progress toward financial independence. You don't, for example, want unemployment or a car accident or a bad back to stop you.

But there's also another less apparent reason for carefully constructing any financial safety nets you want: You want to make sure that the financial safety nets you've set up aren't obstacles to wealth. In other words, while you want to make sure that the safety net is there if you need it, you don't want your financial safety nets to so entangle your finances that it becomes impossible for you to move toward financial independence. This chapter talks about both points of view.

TIPS FOR BUYING INSURANCE

The primary element you'll use to create a financial safety net is a handful of carefully considered insurance policies. You'll need to find an honest, clear-thinking insurance agent to help you with this, but let me start by saying that what you really want to do with your insurance policies is protect your earnings and any property you've accumulated and can't afford to lose.

I'm going to talk about both earnings and property insurance in the next sections. Before I do that, however, let me quickly give three rules for buying your insurance—rules that should make it possible for you to find yourself in a happy middle ground where you're adequately protected and wasting little money.

Here's the first rule: When you buy insurance, you want to protect yourself against general risks—like losing your life, your ability to work, or some piece of valuable property. You don't want to protect yourself against specific events—like developing a bad back, getting cancer, or having a meteorite hit your home.

This first rule seems a bit vague at first blush, but if you think about it a bit, you'll find it's really the one approach that makes sense. By insuring against general risks—like loss of life, ability to earn an income, and loss of property—you don't have to think up all the different ways you can lose your life, your income-earning ability, or some piece of property. If you're buying medical insurance, for example, you want a policy that covers anything medical. You don't want a policy that covers just, for example, cancer. The reason for this is obvious. Your cancer policy is useful only if you get cancer. But it won't do you any good if you break your leg or have complications in a pregnancy or develop a bad back. So that's rule number one.

Here's the second rule: You don't want to buy insurance for risks you can afford to bear. This point often makes most sense if you think about insurance as a financial safety net. For some risks, you don't need a financial safety net because, financially, the risk isn't much of a risk at all. One really good and rather emotional example of this concerns life insurance for children. I love my kids. And I would without reservation sacrifice my life to save theirs. But losing a child, while perhaps an emotional crisis without equal, is not a financial risk. In fact, raising a child is so expensive that, heaven forbid, if something ever did happen to your son or daughter, you'd actually end up in better shape financially than if they lived. Now, please don't misunderstand me. I'm not saying that a child's death isn't a terrible thing. It is. What I am saying is that losing a child isn't a financial disaster. It's an emotional disaster. So it doesn't make sense to construct a financial safety net.

I need to mention a third rule for buying insurance, too: Don't double-insure. Redundant insurance coverage doesn't add to your coverage because you won't be able to collect on more than one policy. Accordingly, you're only wasting the money you spend on the second insurance policy's premium.

So, those are the three rules:

- Insure against general risks, not against specific events.
- Don't buy insurance for risks you can afford to bear yourself.
- Don't double-insure.

Now maybe you're saying to yourself that these three rules don't seem particularly insightful or useful. But in the paragraphs that follow I'll show you that together they will do two things. With a good insurance agent's help, they will let you create a financial safety net that actually increases your chances of successfully running your investment wealth program. Second, they will probably help you find ways to save on insurance premiums, which will provide additional money for your investment wealth program.

EARNINGS INSURANCE

Your biggest asset is your ability to earn an income. Even someone who makes minimum wage will probably earn half a million dollars or more over his or her lifetime. Clearly, then, the first thing you need to think about is protecting your income. And to do this, you basically use two types of insurance: life insurance and disability insurance.

The first policy people typically go get is a life insurance policy. As you probably know, a life insurance policy pays a death benefit to someone if you die. Some life insurance policies also include an investment feature when you pay a larger premium but some of the extra insurance premium goes into a savings account and earns interest.

In thinking about life insurance, the first question you need to ask yourself is whether you even need a policy. Now, of course you're going to die someday. We all will. But in buying a life insurance policy, what you're really purchasing is earnings replacement. In other words, what you're really buying is a policy that will replace your earnings if you die and therefore won't continue to earn. This perspective, by the way, makes it really easy to determine whether in fact you should buy life insurance. You only have to answer a simple question: Is there someone else who depends on my income? If you answer this question "no," then you almost always don't need life insurance. In fact, the only time you'd answer this question "no" and still possibly need life insurance has to do with special estate tax planning problems of the wealthy—something I'll talk about more in Chapter 7, "Odds and Ends." If you answer this question "yes," then you almost always need life insurance.

If you die but your death doesn't mean financial hardship for someone else—say, because you don't have a family or a spouse or whatever—then you won't need insurance. If you die and you have a family but your family wouldn't need your earnings to go on—say, because you're already retired or because you're already financially independent—then you don't need life insurance. You see the pattern, right? The basic idea behind life insurance is that you use it to replace your earnings because somebody else depends on those earnings.

Note, too, that this view of life insurance as simply a tool you can use to replace your earnings means that it's pretty easy to come up with an appropriate life insurance amount. You simply want a big enough policy that your family can invest the life insurance proceeds in something safe and secure and then draw out a monthly amount equal to the earnings you would have provided over the years you would have worked.

Insight

Use the LIFE INSURANCE CALCULATOR from the companion CD to estimate the amount of life insurance you need to replace your earnings. To do so, follow these steps:

STEP 1   Start the Life Insurance Calculator in the same manner as you start any Windows or Macintosh program.

STEP 2   Enter the gross monthly income you want to replace into the **Gross monthly income** box.

STEP 3   Enter the work expenses that are currently paid out of the gross monthly income—what you enter in step 2—into the **Monthly work expenses** box.

STEP 4   Enter the Social Security benefits your dependents will receive into the **Social Security survivors benefits** box.

STEP 5   Enter the years during which you want to replace your income into the **Years of replacement income needed** box.

STEP 6   Enter an estimate of the interest rate your estate will earn on the life insurance proceeds into the **Interest rate** box. For example, if the life insurance proceeds will earn 6 percent annually, enter 6. Note that because what your heirs will need is stable, constant income, you should assume the life insurance proceeds will be invested in conservative income investments, such as bonds.

Insight (continued)

STEP 7   Enter an estimate of the annual inflation rate over the years you want to replace income into the **Inflation rate** box.

STEP 8   Click the **Estimate** button, and the Life Insurance Calculator estimates the monthly income you want to replace, the present value of the income you want to replace, and the rounded-up present value of the income you want to replace. The present value of the income you want to replace equals the life insurance proceeds your dependents will need to replace your income over the stated number of years, assuming that your interest rate and inflation rate estimates are accurate or at least conservative. The rounded-up present value equals the suggested amount of term life insurance you need.

STEP 9   Optionally, click the **Print** button to print a permanent copy of your calculation results.

By the way, if you do go out and try to buy a life insurance policy, you're going to be asked whether you want a term policy or a cash-value policy. A cash-value policy combines a term policy with an investment, or savings account. After paying, in effect, for the term policy that provides the life insurance benefit, the extra money left over goes into a savings account. The cash-value policy is also known by names like whole-life and universal-life. What you want in almost all cases is a term policy—specifically, a renewable term policy. In other words, you want straight insurance.

While people often get confused trying to choose between term insurance and cash-value insurance, the reasons why it's almost impossible for a cash-value policy to represent a good deal are simple as long as you remember that cash-value insurance really just combines term insurance and an investment. Here's the first reason: When you do buy a cash-value policy, a big chunk and sometimes all of the investment part of the premium payment goes to pay a commission to the agent selling you the policy. In comparison, if you invest money into a no-load mutual fund, you pay no sales commission, so all of your money goes into your investment account.

A second reason why cash-value insurance policies typically don't make sense is that the premium you pay is not typically tax deductible. So, there's no subsidy. If you take $1,000 out of your disposable, after-tax income to pay into an IRA or 401(k), you may get tax savings and employer matching of as much as another $500 or even $1,000. In comparison, if you take $1,000 out of your disposable, after-tax income, you typically get no tax savings and no employer matching.

If you take just these first two reasons and look at the effect they might have on your investment portfolio over the first five years, you see why it's basically impossible for a cash-value policy to keep up:

Table A

| | | INVESTMENT PORTFOLIO VALUE | |
YEAR	YOU PAY OUT OF POCKET	INVESTING WITH A CASH-VALUE POLICY	INVESTING WITH AN IRA
1	$1,000	None—your premium pays commission	$1,500
2	$1,000	None—your premium pays commission	$3,100
3	$1,000	$1,000	$5,000
4	$1,000	$2,100	$7,000
5	$1,000	$3,300	$9,200

NOTE: Assumptions: (1) All of investment portion goes to pay commission over first two years and there is no commission paid in year three and beyond. (2) Investment account earns 10 percent annually on a tax-deferred basis, with investment account balances rounded to the nearest $100.

You see the difference, right? In year five, you've got roughly $3,000 in the investment account of the cash-value life insurance policy and roughly $9,000 in your IRA. Why the difference? It's pretty simple. With the IRA, you don't have to pay any sales commission. By *not* paying a big sales commission, you start out with a higher balance, and that means you start compounding interest earlier. What's more, with an IRA, you effectively boost your savings by getting tax savings—roughly $500 a year—that you can also add to your investment account. Note, by the way, that the interest earnings of a cash-value insurance policy are tax-deferred.

But I need to mention something else about cash-value life insurance policies, too. In many cases, the money you invest doesn't go into ownership-type investments. In essence, the money goes into loaner-ship investments. Predictably and fairly, when this is the case, the long-term average annual interest rate you earn on a cash-value insurance policy can't keep up with a stock mutual fund. Chapter 2 talks about why this is the case, remember.

Now out of fairness, I need to say that cash-value life insurance may make sense for people with large estates. If you're an individual with an estate greater than $625,000 or you're married and as a couple your estate is greater than $1,300,000, your heirs may benefit if you purchase cash-value life insurance because it can be used to pay estate taxes. Note, however, that there are actually many powerful techniques available to you for reducing estate taxes. So if your estate will be subject to estate taxes, what you really need to do is consult with an estate planning expert and a tax attorney so that you can review all your options. In order to use cash-value life insurance as an estate planning tool, the policy and your estate plan must be set up just right. Note, too, that over the next few years, the size of estate that you can pass to your heirs without paying estate taxes gradually rises to $1,000,000 for a single person and $2,000,000 for a married couple.

If you understand the reasons why cash-value life insurance policies typically don't make sense and you still think that a cash-value policy or universal-life policy makes sense, you really may be getting a good deal. If you've got a good, trustworthy insurance agent and he or she has said something along the lines of "Well, yeah, cash-value insurance often is a crummy deal for people, but your situation is unique," I would follow your agent's advice. My main point concerning cash-value life insurance is that you want to avoid wasting money on a cash-value life insurance policy that isn't an appropriate choice for you. And you can rather easily waste money on cash-value insurance that could have been better used to fund an investment wealth program.

By the way, the National Insurance Consumer Organization (NICO) will, for $30, analyze a cash-value insurance policy you're considering. If you would like this service, send a copy of the policy proposal, the filled-out application, a check, and a stamped, self-addressed envelope to NICO, 121 N. Payne Street, Alexandria, VA 22314.

But that's enough talk about life insurance, we need to discuss the other form of earnings insurance designed to replace earnings: disability insurance. As noted earlier, your major financial asset is probably your ability to earn a living. You'll probably earn a million dollars or more over your lifetime. And while life insurance protects your family from the risk of losing this income because you die, you still bear another risk: that some injury or illness will force you to quit working before you're financially independent. One out of every three people will be incapacitated for ninety days or more before they reach age sixty-five.

To mitigate this risk, you need to secure some long-term disability insurance. What you want is a long-term policy that after a three-month or six-month waiting period pays you monthly benefit amounts that let you and your family keep going. You'll use a rainy-day fund, described a little later in the chapter, to get through the three-month or six-month waiting period.

Ideally, you want to get a disability policy that protects you against the risk that you'll be unable to work in your own field. If you're an accountant, for example, you want your disability policy to consider you disabled if you can't perform accounting. Without this feature, by the way, you won't get disability if there's some job, any job, you can do. If you can push a broom for minimum wage, for example, you may not receive benefits.

You can also purchase a policy with residual benefits, which means you can return to work. This may add 20 percent to the cost of the policy, but it's worth it. You should also purchase a noncancelable contract, which simply means the policy can't be canceled—say, because you get sick.

Unfortunately, you may find it difficult to get long-term disability insurance. But don't let that discourage you. You need to work with your insurance agent. And note that trade associations and professional societies often offer long-term group disability policies to their members. For example, I belong to the American Institute of Certified Public Accounts, a professional society for accountants. And through my membership, I acquired a long-term disability policy that for just over $100 a year in premiums would pay me $5,000 a month in tax-free benefits after a six-month waiting period for the rest of my life should I become disabled.

One thing to note about disability insurance is that you won't be able to replace all of your income. In other words, if you make, for example, $3,000 a month, you may only be able to get a policy paying $1,800 a month in benefits. That's not great, but it's not as bad as it sounds. For one thing, as long as you pay the disability premiums yourself rather than having an employer pay them, your benefits aren't taxable. And not having to pay income taxes or payroll taxes out of your benefit amount will save you quite a bit of money—probably at least 10 percent, easily 30 percent, and sometimes even as much as 50 percent. In the case of someone making $3,000 a month, for example, income and payroll taxes would probably take at least $300. For most people, income and payroll taxes would take $800 or $900 a month. And someone making $3,000 a month and married to a spouse making a high salary might actually lose almost $1,500 a month to income and payroll taxes. What's more, if you stop working, you won't have any work expenses like commuting.

Social Security

Before you and I wrap up this discussion of earnings insurance, let's talk if ever so briefly about Social Security disability and survivors benefits. If you've worked long enough to have coverage, Social Security may affect the type and amount of life and disability coverage you need.

Let's talk about survivors benefits first. They come into play if you die and have young children. Usually unless you're very young, if you've worked twenty quarters within the past ten years, your children may be eligible for some pretty substantial survivors benefits. The exact hours of work credit you need depends on your age and the year of your disability. And the rules for survivors benefits eligibility change, which unfortunately makes planning for them or counting on them very difficult, but it's quite likely that your children's guardian will receive several hundred dollars a month per child—perhaps even as much as $2,100 a month. This tax-free money may reduce the amount of life insurance coverage you need. Or you may just want to consider it a cushion. But nevertheless, you should be aware that it's there.

If you want to get an idea what sort of survivors benefits your children might be eligible for, your best bet is just to call your local Social Security office or make an appointment to see someone there.

Social Security disability benefits, in my opinion, are more tenuous and as such probably shouldn't be considered as you secure disability coverage. The problem is that the Social Security Administration's definition of disability is extremely strict. If you're middle-aged or younger—so attorneys who practice in this area tell me—it's nearly impossible to get disability benefits unless there is nothing that you can do to earn a wage. And that means, as one attorney told me, you basically have to be a vegetable. If you can push a broom even though you've got a terrible back, for example, you reportedly won't get Social Security disability benefits. If you can stand at a counter and ask, "Do you want fries with your order?" even though a repetitive stress injury means you can't dress yourself, you reportedly won't get benefits.

I should mention that the attorneys I've talked to say that the strictness of the Social Security disability definition becomes less severe the older you get. However, I don't think you want to rely on Social Security disability coverage as you think about purchasing disability coverage. Until the point you reach financial independence, you probably just want to buy as much long-term disability coverage as the insurer will allow.

Saving Money on Earnings Insurance

Most of the earlier discussion focuses on the earnings insurance that you need to provide one part of your financial safety net. Once you understand the need for such a safety net and how to build one, however, you want to look at ways to save money on things like your life insurance and disability coverage.

Regarding life insurance, for example, you want to make sure first that you even need life insurance. Many people buy life insurance even though they have no dependents relying on their earnings. And that's almost always a mistake. If you do this, all you're really doing is enriching your heirs. It makes more sense to enrich yourself by funneling the money you would have spent on premiums into a tax-deductible, tax-deferred investment option like a 401(k) or IRA.

Another thing to note is that, over time, you should need less life insurance. And at some point, you should typically let your term life insurance lapse. Of course, if you've still got kids at home or in school, this isn't the case. But at the point where you've paid a mortgage, accumulated a substantial rainy-day fund, and largely funded your retirement savings, you typically don't need life insurance. If the worst financial thing that can happen is that your spouse keeps working or starts working a bit, that's not all that significant a risk. And while I don't want to sound too macabre here, at the point you or I quit working, our children and spouse by definition don't depend on our earnings anymore. In fact, if you or I do die after we quit working, our families or spouses actually probably end up in better shape because there's one less person to feed, clothe, pay doctors' bills for, and so forth. As noted earlier, some high-net-worth individuals can use cash-value life insurance as an estate planning tool. But in this case, the insurance isn't earnings insurance. It's something different, as your attorney will explain if this is applicable in your situation.

Finally, if you've been investing via a cash-value insurance policy, you may be able to significantly better your financial situation by replacing the cash-value policy with a combination of term insurance and additional contributions to a 401(k), a 403(b), or even an IRA. Unfortunately, if you've been participating in a cash-value insurance policy for a few years, answering the questions how and when you should swap becomes very tricky. So if you find yourself in this situation, contact NICO—I describe how to do this earlier in the chapter—and ask them to analyze your policy to see if it makes more sense just to cash out and then cancel the thing.

The cost savings tactics just mentioned can easily put you on the road to financial independence without reducing your standard of living one iota and without causing you or your family to shoulder unbearable risk.

MEDICAL INSURANCE

It's really tough, unfortunately, to say what you should do about medical insurance. The political and regulatory landscape is so volatile and fast-changing that it's dangerous and well-nigh impossible for me to provide useful, general advice.

For example, what I used to say to people was that they should acquire a major medical policy that stipulated large deductibles. And this advice used to make good sense. The logic of this approach was that you'd pay small monthly premiums yourself—perhaps less than $100 or $200 a month for a family of four—and pretty much all of your doctor and drug bills. But—and this is where the insurance came into play—if you ever found yourself in the situation where a family member needed an expensive operation or was badly injured, you would be covered. So, just to put things into perspective, you'd pay for a $200 office visit yourself. But you'd never have to worry, financially at least, about a $30,000 coronary bypass operation or a $250,000 bone marrow transplant. This strategy meant you were covered for your big medical risks—and even better, it meant that you usually saved money because the amounts you saved on medical premiums more than made up for the out-of-pocket costs you paid yourself.

I also used to suggest that people, even young families, consider not purchasing medical insurance with pregnancy benefits. The reasoning behind this suggestion was that as long as you had insurance that covered a complication from pregnancy and that covered a newborn baby, you were really buying insurance for something that isn't all that expensive. Oh, I know. A normal pregnancy and regular delivery can cost, all totaled, maybe $6,000. And a cesarean delivery maybe doubles this amount to $12,000. But if adding pregnancy benefits to a family's medical insurance costs $500 a month, or almost $6,000 a year, you don't actually save any money even if you're having a baby every year. And you're really not saving a bunch of money except if you're having a baby every year by cesarean delivery. In any other situation, you typically paid way, way more in pregnancy benefits than you could ever hope to receive in paid claims.

I still think you need to think this way a bit. I mean, you want to make sure that you're covered for the really big risks. For example, you want to make sure that you can get the $250,000 operation should you need it. And you want to shoulder the burden of financial risks you can afford to bear. It doesn't make much sense to spend $100 in premiums so you can avoid a $100 medical claim.

But what makes sense also depends on who you are and where you live. For example, in some places like the state I live in, you can paradoxically buy medical insurance after the fact. For example, eight months into a pregnancy, you can reportedly buy medical insurance that provides pregnancy benefits and then cancel the policy after the delivery. I don't think such a tactic is ethical, by the way. It exploits the insurance company's policyholders. I also don't think it makes sense financially because it requires you to bear significant risks. But these sort of weird insurance-buying wrinkles mean that you really need to find a good insurance agent and get his or her input. That input should help you determine which gambits make good sense economically.

To wrap this up, what I suggest you do is talk with an insurance agent or even directly with a medical insurance company (like your state's Blue Cross or Blue Shield insurer) and ask two questions: One, what happens if I need the big operation? Two, do I really save money by having this particular policy? First and foremost, of course, you want to make sure that you do indeed get the big operation if you need it. And then, hopefully, you want to save money by buying a particular insurance policy or by joining a particular health-care plan. Let me also give you a handful of tips:

- Consider a major medical policy as a way to keep your premium costs down but still avoid the financial risk of a big medical catastrophe.

- Look for insurers who have negotiated preferred provider agreements with doctors and hospitals in your area. Typically, these agreements mean that you'll pay less money even for your out-of-pocket expenses and unreimbursed claims.

- Don't buy insurance from some company that may go out of business, because you may not be insurable or as insurable the next time you apply for a policy. This sounds obvious, but what this means is that you buy not only from a company that's large and established but also large and established in your state. In my home state, for example, a large, well-known insurance company started selling medical insurance policies to people and then a year or two later decided not to do business in the state anymore. People with existing medical conditions had real problems getting replacement insurance.

- Look closely at individual policies even when they're more expensive than group policies if you're not sure that you'll always be a member of the group. The problem of getting medical insurance through your employer's group policy, for example, is that you will eventually lose your insurance at some point after you leave work. Note that you can generally opt to continue medical coverage under an employer's group medical policy for eighteen months after you leave the employer.

- Don't cancel one medical insurance policy until you've first secured a replacement policy. You don't want to cancel even a bad policy, for example, if the alternative is that you end up uninsured.

One related comment about all of this stuff: If you do go with a major medical insurance policy, you'll want to quickly accumulate enough money in your rainy-day fund so you can pay the deductible or co-payment amount if need be. I talk about rainy-day funds a bit later in the chapter.

PROPERTY INSURANCE

Property—the stuff you own—is the other major asset you need to consider insuring. You need property insurance for two important reasons. The most obvious reason is that some accident or catastrophe may damage the property—and bearing the risk of such damage yourself is imprudent. For example, if a fire burns down your house, can you afford the loss? Or if someone steals your car, can you afford the loss? In most cases, the answer is no. And in fact, if you've borrowed money to buy a house or car, the lender usually requires you to insure the car or house against this kind of property damage.

But there's also another reason you get property insurance. You want to make sure that your property doesn't damage somebody else or somebody else's property. If a big tree in your backyard falls on the neighbor's house—or on your neighbor—you may be liable for the damages. If you run your car into something or someone, you're probably liable for the damages.

The general rule is that you want adequate insurance to cover both sets of possibilities. For example, you want enough insurance to pay for repairs to your property. And you want enough insurance to pay for repairs to someone else's property.

This all makes sense, right? It's pretty straightforward.

Here's the problem. Typically—and especially in the case of automobile insurance—there's a bunch of other coverage that gets added to your policy. I have to tell you that people debate about whether some of this additional coverage is valuable or appropriate. But—for the sake of full and fair disclosure—I want to at least alert you to the categories of insurance that many people choose not to buy when—and this is important—they've already got appropriate life, disability, and medical insurance policies in force.

Let's start with the least controversial: towing insurance. You don't pay that much for this service. Maybe $50 or $100 a year. But do you ever use it? Do you have duplicate towing insurance coverage with an automobile club or from the automobile manufacturer? If you answer the first question "No" or the second question "Yes," you're probably wasting your money. You would be better off using the $50 or $100 a year in your investment wealth program.

That was easy enough, so let's move on to something a bit more controversial: the medical insurance rider that appears on many auto policies. You'll need to ask your agent for details, but there's a pretty good chance that you're paying for some extra medical insurance as part of your automobile insurance. If someone riding in your car is injured in an automobile accident, this extra medical insurance may pay claims. That sounds like a good idea. But remember what I said at the very beginning of the chapter? Remember that point about not buying duplicate coverage? You're paying two premiums, but you'll only collect on the claim once. So you may be wasting money. In many cases, it makes more sense just to get a good major medical policy, build up your rainy-day fund, and then if you still have leftover savings use that money to fund your investment wealth program. You'll probably save around $75 a year by doing this.

One potential drawback concerning dropping the medical insurance rider on your auto policy concerns the special case when you give other people outside of your family rides. Some people say you should provide medical insurance via your automobile policy to these other people just in case they don't have medical insurance themselves.

You just need to make the call on this. Do you want to add money to your wealth? Or do you want to pay for insurance for some uninsured friend just in case he or she gets hurt in your car?

Another more controversial, cost-saving technique related to your automobile is uninsured and underinsured motorists insurance. In most states you can drop the uninsured or underinsured motorists coverage, and in doing so, you'll save between $100 and $200 a year.

You need to ask your insurance agent for specific details, but in some states what uninsured and underinsured motorists coverage amounts to is bodily injury insurance you buy to cover yourself in the event that an uninsured or underinsured motorist runs into your car. That sounds complicated, but let me explain. Let's say that somebody without insurance or financial resources runs into your car. The property insurance elements of your auto policy—specifically the collision or comprehensive damage clauses—mean that your insurance company will pay for the damage done to your car. In other words, it won't matter that the other motorist doesn't have coverage. If this seems confusing, think of the case where a tree falls on a car or an animal runs out in front of the car. Neither the tree nor the wild animal has insurance coverage, but you're still covered.

What won't be covered by your auto policy's collision and comprehensive clauses, however, is bodily damage to you. In other words, if some uninsured motorist runs into you, thereby destroying your car and killing you, your auto policy's collision and comprehensive clauses will pay for the damage to the auto. But your heirs won't get anything else.

However, if you're killed or disabled in the accident by this other uninsured or underinsured motorist and you have uninsured and underinsured motorist coverage, you or your estate can often sue the motorist and then, if you win your lawsuit, get your insurance company to pay the damages.

This whole business seems to make sense on its face, but I would say if you've got appropriate life, disability, and medical insurance, uninsured and underinsured motorist coverage is redundant. And that means you may want to forgo this coverage. Or you may want to forgo the coverage and instead add more life, disability, or medical coverage.

Now, some people disagree with this position. A personal injury attorney I know says that I'm crazy to even suggest people consider forgoing this coverage. He proudly tells me that he's collected several large awards related to accidents caused by uninsured motorists. But this is a bit like saying you heard about somebody who's won the lottery and that means you should play, too.

The bottom line? Ask your insurance agent to discuss whether this coverage is redundant in light of your insurance policies. And, just as important, make sure that you aren't forgoing some other, more important form of insurance—like disability insurance—and that you aren't cutting corners someplace else, such as not having enough life insurance by spending money on uninsured motorist insurance.

One final point I'll make about spending, say, $300 a year or $400 a year on this questionable auto insurance is that it's ultimately a trade-off. Buy the insurance and you'll get to make a bodily injury claim against an uninsured motorist who causes an accident you're in. Skip the insurance and instead invest the money into a tax-deductible, tax-deferred investment account and you might end up with $75,000 more in your IRA or $150,000 more in your employer-matched 401(k).

PERSONAL LIABILITY INSURANCE

As your wealth grows, it will become more and more important that you secure a large personal liability umbrella policy. Personal liability policies pay damages and legal defense costs when you or some member of your household harms somebody else or somebody else's property and either the damages aren't covered by another policy, such as your homeowners or auto policy, or the damages exceed the other policy's limits.

Let me explain how this works because this is all pretty scary. Say some poor kid crawls onto your roof, falls off, and then his parents sue you for $1,000,000 because the kid now requires twenty-four-hour medical care for the rest of his life. What will happen is that your homeowners policy will pay probably the first chunk of the damages. This might be the first $100,000, for example. But you'll be on the line for the remainder—unless you've got a personal liability umbrella policy. If you do have a personal liability umbrella policy, it typically pays the excess damages. If you don't have a personal liability umbrella policy, the poor kid's parents can probably go after many of your other assets, such as your house, your non-retirement savings, personal property like cars, and so forth.

One rule of thumb, for example, suggests that you get personal liability coverage equal to the greater of $1,000,000 or twice your net worth. For example, if your net worth is $100,000, get $1,000,000 of coverage. If your net worth is $1,000,000, get $2,000,000 of coverage. I think this rule of thumb is pretty good, but you need to consult with your insurance agent and an attorney if you have one. As with other types of insurance, what you really want to do is make sure you've got a financial safety net that means that you don't lose your financial independence in the blink of an eye because somebody—maybe you—does something stupid or has some terrible luck.

Fortunately, personal liability policies aren't expensive. You can probably pick up $1,000,000 of coverage for around $200 a year or less.

FINAL WARNINGS

I want to quickly make two final critically important points about your insurance. First, you need to make any of your changes with the help and council of a good agent. While the rules that I've given you here are generally accurate and useful, I can't know all of the specifics in your situation. And your specific family situation might mean that you should break one of the insurance-buying rules provided earlier.

I also need to emphasize a second and extremely important point. Before you cancel one insurance policy, you want to have first acquired your replacement policy. Okay, this might seem like compulsive worrying on my part, but you absolutely don't want to cancel one insurance policy before you've secured another, better policy. I want to repeat that: Don't cancel one policy until you've secured its replacement. Please. Note that this is true for any type of insurance you need: life, disability, medical, property, or personal liability.

RAINY-DAY FUNDS

One of the quirks related to saving money by reducing your insurance coverage is that while you've reduced the amount you'll pay out in premiums, you've also increased the claims or damages you'll now need to pay out of pocket. For example, while bumping your deductible limit on a medical insurance policy might save you several hundred dollars a month in premiums, you'll end up paying more of your medical costs yourself. For this reason, you'll want to create a personal insurance company using a rainy-day fund. Specifically, take the first money you save by applying the tips or techniques described in this chapter or gleaned from discussions with an insurance agent and store it in an easily accessible, high-interest-bearing money market fund or account.

You'll want to continue adding to your rainy-day fund until you've got plenty of money for paying insurance deductibles and co-payment and co-insurance amounts, for getting through the inevitable period of unemployment, and in a pinch for getting through a disability policy's waiting period. If you add up these amounts, you find that you'll typically want to amass quite a substantial rainy-day fund. Probably thousands and thousands of dollars. But don't get discouraged. The insurance savings techniques I've described in this chapter may allow you to save several hundred dollars a month. You may be able to save $500 a month just by switching to a major medical insurance policy, for example. These savings should allow you to quickly build a rainy-day fund. And, of course, once you've set up your rainy-day fund, you can use any further savings for your investment wealth program.

Insight

Use the RAINY-DAY FUND CALCULATOR from the companion CD to estimate the size of the rainy-day fund you need. To do so, follow these steps:

STEP 1   Start the Rainy-day Fund Calculator in the same manner as you start any Windows or Macintosh program.

STEP 2   Enter your weekly take-home pay into the **Weekly take-home pay** box.

STEP 3   Enter the weekly unemployment benefits to which you'll be entitled if you lose your job into the **Weekly unemployment benefits** box.

STEP 4   Enter an estimate of how long you would be unemployed if you lost your job into the **Weeks of unemployment** box. For example, one rule of thumb says to expect one month of unemployment for every $10,000 of salary. If you make $40,000 a year and apply this rule, you might estimate four months, or roughly sixteen weeks of unemployment.

STEP 5   Enter the amount of your family's total medical insurance deductible into the **Medical insurance deductible** box.

STEP 6   Enter the amount of automobile insurance deductible into the **Auto insurance deductible** box.

STEP 7   If you have other insurance polices with large deductibles, total these deductible amounts and then enter the total into the **Other deductible amounts** box.

STEP 8   Click the **Estimate** button, and the Rainy-day Fund Calculator estimates the rainy-day funds you need for a period of unemployment and for

Insight (continued)

the uninsured risks you bear. The total of these two amounts equals the suggested rainy-day fund size.

STEP 9 Optionally, click the **Print** button to print a permanent copy of your calculation results.

SACRIFICES AND TRADE-OFFS

In the preceding chapters, I've said that you can become financially independent by running a simple investment wealth program. I've also said repeatedly that you should be able to easily find the money you need to run such a program. Chapter 2, as you might remember, explains how you can get much and maybe most of the money you need from other sources like the federal and state government and your employer. And then Chapters 3, 4, and 5 provide you with information, insights, and software tools to help you find the rest of the money you need to run an investment wealth program. Quite frankly, the usual case is that by making a smarter decision in one or two important areas—home ownership, borrowing, or insurance—you can find the money required for an investment wealth program. And this means you should find it rather painless and in fact a bit boring to become financially independent.

But the "usual" case isn't going to work for everybody. The more modest your income and the greater the financial baggage you're already saddled with, the tougher it will be to start and run an investment wealth program. You may also be starting your investment wealth program a little late. Unfortunately, if this is your situation—and I hope that I haven't misled you—you're not going to be able to make just one or two wise financial decisions and find the money you need. You will need to make some sacrifices and consider some trade-offs. And that's what we'll talk about in this chapter.

I'm going to describe a handful of gambits you may be able to use to get the money you need for your investment wealth program. This is a bit awkward. We're going to talk about some things that may make both of us a little uncomfortable. But please keep in mind that you don't have to do all of this stuff. You may need to apply only one or two gambits. And remember, too, that you're really making a trade-off: by selecting a particular gambit, you're saying, "I'll change my behavior in this one way or make this one sacrifice to get on the path to financial independence."

LIVE HEALTHY

Here's the first gambit you should consider—make healthy lifestyle choices in one or two areas. You don't even have to kick all your bad habits. I certainly haven't stopped all mine. But making a healthier choice in even one area—in addition to making you feel better—can produce a surprising amount of wealth.

If you stop smoking and you're a pack-a-day smoker, for example, you'll save about $3 a day in many states. Over a month, that's almost $100. And that amount invested in an IRA over one's working years grows to hundreds of thousands of dollars. If the savings are instead invested in a 401(k) plan with employer matching, that amount might easily grow to over a million dollars over the forty years a person typically works.

If you don't smoke, you probably have other less-than-healthy habits that you can give up or moderate and save similar amounts of money. Do you often come home and open a beer or two? Do you start most days with an expensive specialty coffee? Perhaps a latte or mocha? Do you insist on having meat at every meal? Or a dessert after dinner?

I don't want to sound like a broken record. The suggestion made here isn't that you live a Spartan life devoid of luxury or that you live a life without the occasional indulgence: a cigar, a drink, or a well-aged tenderloin

Insight

Use the COST OF HABIT CALCULATOR from the companion CD to estimate the wealth you lose, or forgo, because of a habit or the wealth you may accumulate because you discontinue a habit. To do so, follow these steps:

STEP 1   Start the Cost of Habit Calculator in the same manner as you start any Windows or Macintosh program.

STEP 2   Enter the amount you regularly spend on your habit into the **I regularly spend this amount** box.

STEP 3   Use the **I spend this amount every** set of option buttons to indicate how often you spend this money: daily, weekly, monthly, or annually.

STEP 4   Enter an estimate of the interest rate you'll earn on your investments into the **Annual interest rate** box. For example, if you think you'll earn 8 percent, enter 8.

STEP 5   Enter an estimate of the years you'll save and invest into the **Years of investing** box.

STEP 6   Enter an estimate of your marginal income tax rate—the top tax rate you pay, including federal, state, and local income taxes—into the **Marginal income tax rate** box. Most middle-class taxpayers, for example, pay top federal tax rates of either 15 percent or 28 percent. High-income taxpayers pay top federal tax rates of 31 percent, 36 percent, or 39.6 percent. State and local tax rates need to be added to the federal tax rates.

STEP 7   Enter the matching percentage your employer will contribute to your savings into the **Employer's matching percentage** box.

STEP 8   Use the **Tax-deductible** option buttons—**Yes** and **No**—to indicate whether you can invest additional money using a tax-deductible investment choice, such as an IRA or a 401(k).

STEP 9   Use the **Tax-deferred** option buttons—**Yes** and **No**—to indicate whether you will be taxed on the income that a taxable investment produces as the income is earned.

Insight (continued)

STEP 10 Click the **Estimate** button, and the Cost of Habit Calculator estimates the wealth you forgo because you choose to continue spending money on a habit—or the wealth you may accumulate because you discontinue a habit.

STEP 11 Optionally, click the **Print** button to print a permanent copy of your calculation results.

steak. But the reality is that if we turn any of these items into a habit, not only do we sacrifice our health, we also spend a lot of money. For fun, I created a little table that estimates the daily or weekly cost of particular habits and the amount you might easily accumulate in something like an IRA by quitting today and investing your savings over the next thirty years.

Table B

HABIT	COST	LOST WEALTH
Smoking a pack a day	$3/day	$250,000
Buying a specialty coffee every morning	$2/day	$167,000
Drinking two six-packs of beer weekly	$10/week	$119,000
Having a gourmet cookie with lunch	$1/day	$83,000

NOTE: The assumption is that you invest your daily or weekly savings over a thirty-year period of time using a tax-deductible, tax-deferred investment account (such as an IRA), that you invest the savings related to the tax deduction (28 percent), and that you earn a 10 percent annual rate of return.

Let me mention one other quick thing about this "make a healthy lifestyle choice." One practical aspect of this gambit is that it's easy to apply. For example, if you decide just to quit smoking in order to save

some money, that's it. You don't need to be tracking every penny you save or spend to confirm the savings. Stop smoking, and you're there. The same thing holds true for the after-work beers you enjoy. Or the ice cream. One decision does it.

BECOME ENVIRONMENTALLY AWARE

Here's another neat way to save money. Just become more environmentally aware. If you do the things suggested by ecologists—reduce, reuse, and recycle—you save money. For Americans particularly, this is often a tough gambit to apply practically. If some item breaks, we're tempted to replace it rather than repair it. If the kids need new clothes, we often don't first scout out a garage sale or visit a thrift shop. But if you can disconnect yourself from the consumption-oriented lifestyle of your neighbors, you'll not only be taking better care of mother earth, you'll save a lot of money.

Take, for example, your next car purchase decision. If you do something like get a small, fuel-efficient station wagon rather than one of those big, gas-guzzling sport utility vehicles, you'll very likely save around $750 in gasoline a year. If you invest this money, including any tax savings, over thirty years in something like an IRA, you end up with roughly $180,000. If you can instead stash this same money into an employer-sponsored 401(k) plan with 50 percent matching, you end up with roughly $260,000.

The average family can probably save around a couple hundred bucks a year by turning the thermostat down and driving the speed limit. These savings, plowed into an IRA, might grow to around $45,000 over thirty years. And they would grow close to $70,000 if plowed into a 401(k) plan with 50 percent matching.

Saving $250 a year in clothing costs by shopping first at secondhand stores would probably let you accumulate around $60,000 in an IRA and almost $90,000 in the right 401(k).

You may not want to do any of this stuff, of course. If you're looking

at buying a car, a station wagon probably isn't as cool or whatever as a big sport utility vehicle. You may not want to wear a sweater around the house. And the idea of buying secondhand stuff may strike you as distasteful. But if you do choose one or more of these tactics, not only do you get to save money—and quite a bit at that—but you also pollute less.

THINK BIG PICTURE

Okay, this is probably the most awkward area for us to discuss. But thoroughness demands that I point out that your big life decisions typically have the biggest financial impacts.

For example, if you decide to get married to the right person—somebody who is stable and honest and hardworking—your partnership almost certainly generates immensely positive financial effects. Two people working together, saving together, sharing a home amount to a powerful economic unit. So that's good.

Conversely, if you decide to marry some clown who isn't stable or honest or hardworking, your mate can easily become a real financial burden and an insurmountable obstacle to financial independence. Now, please understand me. I'm not saying that you shouldn't marry Bob or Bernice or whatever your partner's name is. What I am saying is that should you marry someone with, for example, a substance abuse problem, you'll find it nearly impossible to become financially independent by running an investment wealth program. If you shack up with someone who has some other destructive, compulsive behavior—gambling, shopping, eating, or anything else—you'll again find it very challenging to become financially independent by running an investment wealth program.

Since we're on the topic of marriage, I'm going to point out that divorce is another really big life decision that carries with it huge financial effects. I want to talk in a minute about how you can save money, but first let me review the possible financial impact of divorce.

The best-case scenario, financially speaking, is when you have a divorce that involves no children. In this case, you've got both legal costs

and property liquidation costs to incur. With no children, you can pay as little as a few hundred dollars in an amicable, no-contest divorce. Of course, you can also end up paying all the money you have if you and your spouse have accumulated substantial assets and decide to do things the nasty way.

Even without kids, there's also typically the issue of any property liquidation costs. Financial requirements or even just plain meanness on the part of one or both spouses can result in a couple having to liquidate, or sell off, much of what they own. The costs to sell a home can run to ten percent of the home's value, which often eats up your equity. You'll also typically incur either direct or hidden transaction costs when you sell anything else: a business, car, boats, and any expensive toys. If you don't pay a commission directly, you may still pay one indirectly by having to sell some item for its wholesale value rather than its retail value. And you may also have to spend lots of time and money trying to sell your stuff.

If you add children to the mix, not only do your legal costs jump to several thousand dollars because of the custody agreement, but you'll find yourself dealing with the financial reality of child support: If you pay child support, it'll be almost more than you can afford. And if you receive child support, it won't be nearly enough.

And then there's the hidden cost of children in a divorce. Both parents often go out and find a family-sized house or apartment so there's room for the kids. Which means that while Mom and Dad are making the same amount of money as before the divorce, they're paying to maintain two homes. And that's tough.

The bottom line is that divorce and everything that comes with divorce has a hugely negative impact on your personal finances. I am not in any way suggesting that you stay in a bad marriage with an abusive or dangerous or unfaithful partner for the sake of money.

But what I am pointing out is that divorce, in addition to everything else it is, also typically amounts to a financial disaster. And my observation, as a financial advisor and not a therapist, is that some of the people who get divorced or find themselves on the road to divorce might make a different decision if they truly understood the financial impact of divorce. Another way to say this same thing is that if you've got a marriage or family that's broken, the least expensive and least bad option may just be to try and fix the thing. And in any event, if you are contemplating a divorce or contemplating behavior or decisions that may lead to divorce, you have to include the financial effect of divorce in your analysis. This is particularly true if bad or stressful household finances are a contributing factor in a bad or broken marriage.

If you and your soon-to-be-former spouse are already past the point of no return, let me suggest that you consider the financial aspects of the decisions you'll make. You may want to work with an attorney who believes in and promotes mediation. This may minimize your legal fees. You probably want to get the help of a tax advisor to make sure that you liquidate any assets in an efficient way. This may minimize the tax effects of your divorce.

In particular, I would suggest you do three things related to income taxes. First of all, make sure that you use tax-free rollovers to move money from one spouse's retirement account to the other spouse's retirement account. For example, if your spouse has $20,000 in a 401(k) plan which you get half of as part of the divorce, don't take the $10,000 in cash. Instead, roll the money over into another retirement account, such as an IRA Rollover account. To do this, you direct your ex-spouse's retirement account trustee—the bank or mutual fund company holding the money— to send the money directly to the bank or mutual fund where you've opened the IRA Rollover account. The reason you don't want to take the cash and spend, by the way, is that you'll pay income taxes and penalties on the money if you do, and this will probably eat up as much as half of the money. And if you do attempt to transfer the money, it gets messy because your ex-spouse's trustee will withhold 20 percent—$2,000 of the $10,000 in our example—for income taxes. You'll get this money back if you open a new $10,000 IRA within sixty days, but remember you'll only have an $8,000 check. You'll need to come up with the other $2,000, at least temporarily, yourself.

Here's a second thing you want to consider: If you and your ex-spouse make and will continue to make significantly different incomes and you have a child, consider giving the personal exemptions to the person who makes the most money. Then split the tax benefits. For example, if you make $30,000 and therefore pay income taxes at the 15 percent rate, two personal exemptions for a couple of kids are worth around $750 a year in tax savings. If your ex-spouse makes $150,000 and therefore pays income taxes at the 40 percent rate, two personal exemptions for a couple of kids are worth around $2,000 a year in tax savings. What you guys should do is give the exemptions to the person making $150,000 a year and then split the $1,250 benefit.

Here's a third tax-related tip: If you have two or more children, will share custody of your children, and both you and your spouse make similar and above average incomes, ask your attorney about drafting the custody agreement so that both you and your spouse can file your income tax returns using the favorable head of household filing status. If you and your spouse each make $60,000 a year, you'll together save around $1,500 a year in taxes by doing this. If you and your spouse make $90,000 a year, you'll save around $2,300 a year in taxes. To file your income tax return as a head of household, you'll just need to provide a home and half the support for one of your dependents, such as one of your kids.

Finally, as you move past the divorce—and this will be hard—you need to be really careful about attempting to salve the emotional trauma of your divorce with money. I know it's hard. But you want to be careful—for your sake.

HUNT FOR ELEPHANTS

Here's a more abstract gambit you can use to find the money necessary to run an investment wealth program: Look for savings in your biggest expense categories.

The point here is that if you want to find, for example, $50 of monthly savings, it's often a lot easier to locate those savings in some category where you're spending $500 a month or $1,000 a month. If you try to save $50 on your monthly grocery bill, for example, you may be able to do so simply. Perhaps all you need to do is go meatless a couple of nights a week. Or maybe you can buy some food items in bulk.

In comparison, if you try to find $50 of monthly savings in some area where you're spending $50 or $100, your cost-cutting measures need to be severe. For example, the only way to save $50 a month out of a $100-a-month category—say it's your electric utilities expense—may be to do something drastic and impractical like stop heating your house or not use the refrigerator.

One other thing I'll say about all this is that I can guess that your largest expenses are probably housing, food, and transportation. And I understand that those areas are places where it's not easy to find savings. Nevertheless, if you are going to locate savings, you've got a much better chance of finding the savings in places where you're already spending a lot of money.

STOP BUYING GAZINGUS PINS

A few years ago, Joe Dominquez and Vicki Robbins wrote a wonderful book called *Your Money or Your Life* (Viking Press, 1992). While the book provides dozens and maybe even hundreds of good ideas for more prudently managing one's personal finances, I found one of their notions especially thought provoking and very applicable to running an investment wealth program.

Dominquez and Robbins suggest that some people have an item—their book labels the item a gazingus pin—that these people habitually and compulsively buy even though the item really isn't needed. Perhaps, for example, purchasing the item is justified as a hobby. I have a friend who buys a weekly CD as part of a jazz music collection. Or maybe purchasing the item is somehow justified because it can be used as a gift. I've known of more than one grandmother who buys toys compulsively. And you even see people misclassify items as investments. The rich do this with art objects all the time.

Now there's nothing wrong of course with hobbies or gifts or art. But as you do look for money to fund an investment wealth program, consider the possibility that you have a gazingus pin habit. If you habitually buy souvenir T-shirts, the latest kitchen appliances, collectible porcelain figurines, or power tools—even though you already have dozens of these items—you may actually be buying gazingus pins. Perhaps without even realizing what you're doing. And if this is the case, you can often save a surprising amount of money every year just by breaking your gazingus pin habit.

STOP USING A CREDIT CARD

I made this point earlier, but let me just repeat it. Some studies show and my nonscientific observation confirms that people spend more when they use a credit card than they do when they use cash or write a check. In other words, even people who don't carry a balance on their credit cards still probably spend more by using a credit card than they would in some other way.

This may seem like a small point. But if you spend an extra 20 percent because you're using a credit card and you only make modest use of the credit card—say you spend $250 a month—using a credit card still costs you $50 a month. This might be the case if, for example, you buy some of your groceries and then most of your family's clothing using the credit card. If you instead plop that $50 a month into an IRA, also plop the tax savings you get from this contribution into the IRA, and then let the savings compound over thirty years, you end up with around $150,000.

KEEP FINANCIAL RECORDS

If you're reading this book, chances are good that you've got a personal computer. Otherwise, how would you use the utilities on the companion

CD, right? So I want to suggest something. If you can't find the money you need to run an investment wealth program in some other way, get one of the popular financial record-keeping programs, also called checkbook programs, like Quicken by Intuit or Microsoft Money. Then start using the program to get good, detailed records of your income and your spending.

For about the price of this book or maybe slightly more, a checkbook program will not only allow you to find extra savings, it will also help you rather effortlessly spend less money. And rest assured: These programs aren't difficult and don't take much time to use.

A checkbook program directly saves you money in some obvious ways. If you keep accurate spending records and a close tab on your bank account balances, you're less likely to bounce a check and incur those nasty insufficient funds fees. You're also more likely to spot erroneous bank charges. These sorts of savings can be significant over a year: Ten dollars here and ten dollars there, and pretty soon you're talking about a lot of money.

A checkbook program also usually indirectly saves you money. Because all of these programs let you easily monitor your spending by category, the programs make it possible to see what you're spending by eating out, by subscribing to magazines, by having insurance, and so forth. This extra awareness of your spending typically produces expense savings almost naturally. When you notice, for example, that you spent eighty bucks last month taking the family to a restaurant they didn't actually enjoy, you may decide to instead visit a good drive-in burger joint this month. When some magazine you haven't read for months comes due for subscription—and you realize you've spent $300 over the last year in magazines and newspapers—you may decide not to renew. When you realize your insurance premium has gone up even though you've had no traffic accidents or citations, you may be more likely to ask your agent about the increase, and that may prompt him to do something that'll save you money, too. He may be able to find some discount you can get. Or, maybe he can find a cheaper insurance company.

Just for the record, I don't think it actually matters all that much which program you use. Having written books on both Quicken and Money, I know both programs rather well. The main thing is that you begin using one of these tools or an equivalent substitute to keep a close watch over your money. It doesn't really matter how much you choose to spend on long-distance telephone charges, magazine subscriptions, or video rentals. But you should know how much you spend on these and other items. And you should make sure that you're spending what you want to spend—and not so much that some expense gets in the way of achieving financial independence.

COMPROMISE

Okay, here's another money-saving idea you may want to consider as a way to fund your investment wealth program. Think about all of the ways you spend money and then select one that, in the grand scheme of things, isn't as important as your investment wealth program. In other words, think about some of the things you buy that aren't actually essential. Then pick something you're willing to trade to get on the road to financial independence.

Maybe, for example, golf isn't all that important to you. Sure. You enjoy the camaraderie and the fresh air. But when you really weigh the fun and benefits of golf as compared to financial independence, what you just might conclude is that you'll be happier in the long run trading golf for wealth. And this might be especially true if you can get some of the benefits of golf, for example, in another way. Maybe you begin to take long walks to get the exercise you previously received from your golf outings. Maybe you volunteer at a local community service club for the fellowship you previously enjoyed as part of golf.

Note, too, that I'm not suggesting you give up golf, for example, if golf is the thing you love most in life. The point is that if you're currently spending money on, for example, gardening, gazingus pins, and golf and if of these three things golf is the least important, you might want to trade it for financial independence. You can use the Cost of Habit Calculator, described earlier in the chapter, to see what financial effect making a compromise has.

Before I wrap up this discussion of picking a compromise, I ought to make one other, perhaps obvious point. If you're going to pick a compromise—and you know this—it needs to be a compromise *you* make and not one you expect your partner or family to make. It's no good and not fair for you or me to decide our kids or spouses can do without some item or activity. If you're looking for compromise that'll fund all or a portion of your investment wealth program, the compromise needs to be one that you will make.

SELL OR GIVE AWAY THE WHITE ELEPHANT

Some people, almost without realizing it, bear the expense of owning and maintaining some expensive and largely unproductive asset: an extra car that's rarely used, a boat, some expensive gadget or piece of equipment, and so on. The weird thing about these sorts of white elephants is that they in themselves can be an obstacle to financial independence and an investment wealth program. Take the case of a family who keeps an old vehicle—perhaps because it wasn't worth much at trade-in anyway. You can imagine how someone decides to keep an old truck for hauling stuff or to hang on to an extra car in case of breakdowns. Maybe the vehicle is only worth a few hundred dollars. And after all, it really does seem handy on occasion to have an extra vehicle.

The problem with this thinking is that there are typically a bunch of other expenses associated with hanging on to and maintaining these sorts of items. With an unnecessary car, you'll have annual license tabs, insurance, and sometimes storage costs. With a larger-than-needed home, you'll have extra taxes, insurance, and typically mortgage interest or rent to pay. With items as innocuous as heirloom furniture you've received as a gift or an expensive piece of jewelry you're afraid to wear, you're still often tying up cash in something that's an emotional asset but a financial liability.

For these reasons, it often does make sense to sell or even give this stuff away. For starters, you'll often get some cash. And even if this is only a few hundred bucks, every little bit helps. And then over the long haul, with less stuff to take care of, you should find it easier to save money on all the direct and indirect costs of holding on to some item.

 **Insight**

Use the **INVESTMENT CALCULATOR** from the companion CD to estimate the wealth you might accumulate by getting rid of some white elephant. To do so, follow these steps:

STEP 1   Start the Investment Calculator in the same manner as you start any Windows or Macintosh program.

STEP 2   Click the **Future balance** option button to indicate that you want to estimate the wealth you might accumulate at some point in the future. The **Future balance** button is part of the **Investment variable to calculate** option button set.

STEP 3   Click the **annually** option button to indicate that you will express any savings you enjoy because you dispose of your white elephant as annual savings. The **annually** button is part of the **Type of payment annuity** option button set.

STEP 4   Enter the amount you will receive from selling your white elephant into the **Initial investment balance** box. If you receive cash for disposing of the white elephant, enter the amount as a positive number. If you will have to pay money for disposing of your white elephant, enter the amount you'll have to pay for disposal as a negative number.

Insight (continued)

STEP 5   Enter an estimate of the years you'll save money by disposing of the white elephant into the **Investment term (in years)** box.

STEP 6   Enter an estimate of the interest rate you'll earn on the savings you invest into the **Annual return on investment** box. For example, if you think you'll earn 10 percent, enter 10.

STEP 7   Enter an estimate of the amount you'll save on an annual basis by disposing of the white elephant into the **Regular investment addition** box.

STEP 8   Click the **Estimate** button, and the Investment Calculator estimates the wealth you may accumulate because you dispose of your white elephant. Note that this calculation actually ignores any tax savings and employer matching benefits you may accrue. Therefore, it probably understates the benefit of disposing of your white elephant.

STEP 9   Optionally, click the **Print** button to print a permanent copy of your calculation results.

FORGO SPENDING YOUR NEXT RAISE (OR WINDFALL)

Sometimes when you can't find any other way to free up extra cash, it works to promise yourself that you'll begin saving the amount of your next raise or that you'll save all of your next windfall. In other words, although you might be sure that you can't find any extra money in your budget today, what you can do is say to yourself, "Self, when I get my annual raise, I'm going to take all of that money and stick it into an IRA or into the company's 401(k) plan." In other words, rather than just spending your increase in pay, you save it instead.

Some people, by the way, point out that if there's inflation, a raise is needed to maintain your lifestyle. This point sounds right on the face of it, but it's often only partially true. And there are a couple of reasons for this. First of all, in all likelihood, the consumer price index (CPI) that employers and the government use to estimate inflation overestimates price increases. Many economists think, for example, that the CPI overstates inflation by as much as 1 percent. That means, then, that if you get a 3 percent cost-of-living adjustment, you might typically have to spend only 2 percent of the raise in order to keep up with inflation. And that would mean you could save some of the cost-of-living adjustment without reducing your living standard.

Take the case of a person making $30,000 a year, for example. In this case, a 3 percent cost-of-living adjustment adds $75 a month to the person's before-tax wages. But it's quite possible that this person's expenses haven't really inflated by $75 a month. They may have only risen by $50. If this person can save rather than spend that extra $25, well, that's money that can go into an investment wealth program.

I should point out, too, that there's another separate reason why the consumer price index may tend to overstate inflation. It's very possible that you've locked in some of your major expenses. For example, if you purchase a home, increases in housing prices, while affecting the CPI, don't bump up your cost of living. That makes sense, right? There's another way to think of this. If your employer gives you a 3 percent cost-of-living adjustment, perhaps attributing 1 percent of this adjustment to housing inflation, you don't actually have to pay extra money for your housing if you've already purchased a home.

For example, returning to the example where a person making $30,000 gets a 3 percent, or $75-a-month, cost-of-living adjustment, it may be that $25 of this adjustment represents a bump in your wages to pay for increased housing expenses. But if you've locked in your housing expenses because you've purchased a home, apartment, or condominium, your housing expenses won't actually rise by $25. So there's another $25 you can use for your investment wealth program.

For the reasons just mentioned, it's very possible that you might receive a 3 percent adjustment but only need to spend, say, 1 percent of the adjustment to keep up your living standard. And the leftover 2 percent can make a big contribution to an investment wealth program.

Think about this for a minute. Say you make $30,000 a year and that you save two-thirds of a 3 percent, or $75-a-month, cost-of-living adjustment. This may mean that you can save $50 a month, or $600 a year, the first year after you get the cost-of-living adjustment. If you get another $75-a-month cost-of-living adjustment next year and you again save $50 a month of this adjustment, this may mean you can save $100 a month, or $1,200, the second year after you get the cost-of-living adjustment. If you save two-thirds of a $75-a-month cost-of-living adjustment the third year, you may be able to save $1,800. If you really did something like this but in years four and beyond just kept your saving amount set to $1,800, you end up with around $130,000 in present-day, uninflated dollars after twenty-five years. That's pretty good.

If you happen to work someplace where your employer provides a 401(k) plan with 50 percent matching, you might be able to boost these amounts even further to $900 the first year, $1,800 the second year, and $2,700 the third year. If you did this but in years four and beyond just kept your saving amount set to $2,700, you end up with around $200,000 in present-day, uninflated dollars after twenty-five years. That's even better.

Note that this notion of siphoning off a portion of your cost-of-living adjustment doesn't have to reduce your standard of living one bit. You can still afford the extra amount you'll pay for groceries and gasoline. All you're really doing is redirecting the portion of your cost-of-living adjustment that you don't need to your investment wealth program.

Another often painless way to come up with money for an investment wealth program is through windfalls. By windfalls, I mean unexpected chunks of money like bonuses, income tax refunds, inheritances, and gifts you receive. It's amazingly easy to piddle these amounts away. You hear, for example, that you're going to get $5,000 you didn't expect. I think many of us are tempted to think first about how we might enjoy spending such a windfall. But if you decide to save such a windfall and save any tax deductions you receive, the ultimate effect can be surprising. In fact, what you can often do is use a windfall to cut five, ten, or even twenty years off of the time it takes you to reach financial independence.

Insight

Use the WINDFALL CALCULATOR from the companion CD to see how much wealth you accumulate by saving rather than spending a windfall you receive. To do this, follow these steps:

STEP 1   Enter the amount of the windfall into the **Windfall amount** box.

STEP 2   Enter the number of years it will take to invest the windfall into the **Years to fully invest windfall** box.

STEP 3   Enter an estimate of the interest rate you'll earn on your investments into the **Annual interest rate** box. For example, if you think you'll earn 8 percent, enter 8.

STEP 4   Enter an estimate of the years you'll save and invest into the **Years of investing** box.

STEP 5   Enter an estimate of your marginal income tax rate—the top tax rate you pay, including federal, state, and local income taxes—into the **Marginal income tax rate** box. Most middle-class taxpayers, for example, pay top federal tax rates of either 15 percent or 28 percent. High-income taxpayers pay top federal tax rates of 31 percent, 36 percent, or 39.6 percent. State and local tax rates need to be added to the federal tax rates.

STEP 6   Enter the matching percentage your employer will contribute to your savings into the **Employer's matching percentage** box.

STEP 7   Use the **Tax-deductible** option buttons—**Yes** and **No**—to indicate whether you can invest additional money using a tax-deductible investment choice, such as an IRA or a 401(k).

Insight (continued)

STEP 8 Use the **Tax-deferred** option buttons—**Yes** and **No**—to indicate whether you will be taxed on the income that a taxable investment produces as the income is earned.

STEP 9 Click the **Estimate** button, and the Windfall Calculator estimates how much wealth you accumulate because you choose to save your windfall rather than spending it.

STEP 10 Optionally, click the **Print** button to print a permanent copy of your calculation results.

If you do receive a windfall, you want to invest the money the same way you invest any other funds. You want to dollar-cost average the money into a tax-deductible, tax-deferred investment and save rather than spend any tax deductions or employer matching you receive. As described in Chapter 2, this approach lets you boost your savings. This approach also lets you reduce the risk that you'll plow a bunch of money into the stock market at a high point or do some other fanciful thing with your money.

Because this can be a bit trickier than you might expect, let me quickly give you an example of how this might work in the case of a $12,000 inheritance you receive. If you wanted to put this money into an IRA at the rate of $2,000 a year, you might think you could just put the $12,000 into a savings account and then withdraw $2,000 every year, placing the $2,000 into an IRA every year for the next six years.

But it's actually not that simple because your $2,000 contributions would actually produce significant tax savings, maybe as much as $800 or $900 a year. So what you'd need to do is set the inheritance aside in a savings account, withdraw $2,000 a year for IRA contributions, but then—and this is important—add back to the special savings account any tax deductions you receive. So, for example, if you got an $800 tax re-fund at the end of the year because you'd made a $2,000 IRA contribution, you would want to deposit the $800 into your special savings account—the one that's providing the money you're using to make your IRA deductions.

If you were using a 401(k) plan, the mechanics work in a slightly different way: Because you make 401(k) contributions from your paycheck, what you would want to do is make the largest possible 401(k) contribution each month. This would make your paycheck smaller. For example, if you made an $800 401(k) contribution each month, your monthly paycheck might be $575 smaller. The reason the paycheck wouldn't be $800 a month smaller is that by reducing your taxable income with 401(k) contributions you would also be reducing your income taxes. But then you'd make up the $575-a-month shortfall by withdrawing money from the special savings account. So what you would do in this case is withdraw another $575 from your special savings account.

Let me make two final comments about saving windfalls. First let me say that when some people hear this, they say things like, "But I want to spend the money!" or "Why shouldn't I enjoy this extra money?" These perspectives are understandable—and very logical. The one thing people need to realize is that by saving the money, they're not depriving themselves. A person does benefit by saving a windfall. Ultimately, he or she will spend the money. What saving windfalls does is, effectively, spread out the benefit of a windfall over the years of your life. And that actually makes a lot of sense. Why take, for example, a $50,000 inheritance and spend it all in one year? Why not spread out the benefit of the windfall in little chunks over, for example, twenty years?

One other final and very quick comment. Often, the best time to make a decision that you'll save a windfall is before you know you're getting the windfall. You'll find it relatively easy to conclude, for example, that you should save windfalls, thereby using them as part of an investment wealth program, tonight after dinner or after the kids head off to bed. If you wait until you know you're getting a bonus, inheritance, or gift—when the possibility of a new boat or minivan or European vacation is very real and very close—it becomes more challenging to exercise discipline.

And this is often true even for people who are normally pretty rational. The euphoria that accompanies some big bonus and the grief that precedes an inheritance may affect our decision making. Enough said.

CREATE YOUR OWN WINDFALL

Let me throw out a quick idea related to the previous point about windfalls. You may be able to create your own windfall. And this is particularly true for people in their forties, fifties, or even sixties. Oftentimes, mature investors—particularly people who haven't been serious investors to date—have valuable assets they can liquidate and then invest in the manner I just described.

Do you have a three-bedroom house even though two of your three kids are already grown? Maybe you can downsize to a two-bedroom condominium and free up $25,000, $50,000, or even $100,000 of extra cash. Note that you no longer pay capital gains taxes on the first $250,000 ($500,000 if you're married) of profit on the sale of a primary residence.

You may have other valuable items, too, that in the grand scheme of things and compared to the importance of achieving financial independence should be turned into cash. A boat or vacation home. An extra vehicle. Expensive furniture, tools, guns, or musical gear. You can shake your head at the plausibility of this notion. You may not want to do it. And I'm just throwing out the idea so that you're aware of all your options. But if you've been working for, say, twenty years and have been making an average salary of $25,000, you've actually made and spent $500,000. And it's very likely that some of this is essentially still hanging around in the form of expensive and valuable items you purchased years ago.

Two final but quick points about this tactic. First, you may have to pay capital gains on the item you sell if it's increased in value since you bought it and tax laws don't say it's okay to exclude the gain or part of the gain. Second, you may be able to augment whatever you net from liquidating some item with income tax savings and 401(k) employer matching contributions.

Because this sounds tricky, let me show you how this works. Let's say, for example, that you've got a vintage electric guitar that you sell for $12,500. If you originally paid, say, $500 for this item, you've actually got a capital gain of $12,000 in this case. This is the difference between the $12,500 sales price and the $500 you originally paid. That may mean you'll pay $2,400 in capital gains taxes, netting $9,600 in actual investable cash.

If you invest this money in an IRA or similar tax-deductible investment and you pay a top combined federal and state income tax rate of 33 percent, you may be able to use the money to invest roughly $14,500. This is because if you invest $14,500, you will save about $4,900 in income taxes, and the $9,600 guitar sales proceeds plus the $4,900 in tax savings equals $14,500. So look what's happened here. By creating a windfall opportunity, you've already turned your $12,500 guitar into $14,500 of investment.

If you happen to invest this money in a tax-deductible investment that includes employer matching, such as a 401(k) or Simple-IRA, you may be able to further augment this money. Obviously, the money you get from such matching depends on the provisions of the employer's plan. But if a plan includes 50 percent matching, you may be able to get the employer to kick in another $7,250 of money for your investment wealth program. And at this point, by creating a windfall opportunity, you turn your $12,500 guitar into almost $22,000.

That amount of money can make a huge difference to your investment wealth program. It jump-starts your savings. And it greatly accelerates your journey to financial independence.

GET A RAISE OR BETTER JOB

I want to leave you with one final idea. If you're having real trouble coming up with any extra money to fund an investment wealth program and you've looked at all the ideas and options laid out thus far, consider the possibility that you need to get active and aggressive about getting a raise or a better job.

Okay, I don't know the specifics of your work situation, of course. I don't know anything about your work habits, productivity, or intellectual prowess. But I do know—just because you're reading this book—that you've got some common sense, that you want to better yourself, and that you're capable of independent learning. And these qualities mean to me that you may be able to say to your employer something like this: "I want to deliver to you, my employer, another $10,000 in value a year in my job. I figure if you, my employer, get to keep $5,000 and then I get an extra $5,000 a year, we're both way ahead."

Does that sound crazy? I don't think it is. I'm not saying you should get a $5,000 raise just because you want one. What if you and your employer can agree on how you can deliver an extra value to your company? What if you work a bit harder every day? Leave fifteen minutes later, for example, and just every day get a bit more work done or develop some special, valuable new project or business opportunity. Or what if you, on your own time, learn some valuable new skill that you can offer to your employer? Maybe you learn about how to exploit some new technology or maybe you learn a foreign language. To summarize, what if you do something that puts another $10,000 or $20,000 of profit into the company's checking account?

You may chafe at my suggestion. Because I'm a business owner, you may scoff at the idea as self-serving. Nevertheless, I stand by my point, which is, fundamentally, that it should be relatively easy for you over a period of months to greatly increase the value you deliver to your employer. And if you do this, you should get paid more money. And even a modest percentage increase in your salary—over and above any other adjustments for things like inflation—can easily fund an investment wealth program. Think about it. How much investment would you need to make in your own development to justify an extra 5 percent next year? Probably not that much. And yet, if you're making $20,000 a year, this extra raise might provide another $1,000 a year for an investment wealth program. If you're making $50,000, this extra raise might provide another $2,500 for an investment wealth program.

This tactic isn't one you can expect to work in a few weeks or a few months, of course. You're really talking about long-term developmental and long-term career growth. But the tactic will work. This is the fundamental reason why some people get paid more money and some people get less.

Let me say one more thing about getting a raise. If you're working someplace where going the extra mile doesn't pay off—perhaps because there's a rigid salary plan in place or collective bargaining agreements in force—maybe you should look at what other employment options you have available. A market-driven economy like ours is ruthlessly efficient. Too often, employees get burned by this efficiency. But there's no reason why you shouldn't instead be rewarded by this efficiency. If you work harder and smarter, if you deliver a richer set of job skills to an employer, and if you're trustworthy, many employers happily and only fairly pay you more money.

SOME CLOSING COMMENTS

This chapter was an awkward one to write. And, my sense is, it's also an awkward one to read. We've spent a bunch of time discussing what sacrifices and trade-offs you can and may need to make to become financially independent.

My hope is that you've found the money you need to run your investment wealth program. And if that's the case, you really ought to feel good about yourself. You're not going to be sorry, I promise you.

There is the possibility, however, that none of the stuff I've talked about here will work for you. And that begs some questions: What should you do if you still can't seem to find the money necessary to run an investment wealth program? What if none of the ideas and options discussed work for you? What if none of the sacrifices and trade-offs make sense for your family?

I want to suggest that your reading hasn't been without profit. You now know what it takes to run an investment wealth program. You understand the decisions that people who become wealthy have to make. If you've decided that you'd rather not become financially independent given the sacrifices you have to make, you've actually gained a truly valuable perspective.

You'll probably have to work much longer than the people who follow the plan described in this book. If you are able to retire someday, you'll almost surely find yourself living more modestly than you do now. But your decision isn't without merit. An Old Testament proverb says you shouldn't begin a journey unless you know the cost and are sure you want to reach the destination. And so you're actually in much better shape philosophically, although not financially, if you know the destination isn't worth the journey.

ODDS AND ENDS

The earlier chapters of this book focus, almost myopically, on how you map out a route to financial independence using an investment wealth program and how you find the money for such a program. I want to shift gears a bit in this chapter by talking about a handful of related topics. This is stuff you need to consider as part and parcel of running an investment wealth program.

PLAN FOR YOUR FINANCIAL INDEPENDENCE IN NONFINANCIAL TERMS

I guess here's the first thing I want to point out. Marching along toward financial independence is all good and well. I wrote this book to help you do this. You're reading this book because you want to do this. But—and you intuitively know this, I'm sure—you need to think about what financial independence means in other than financial terms. If you run an investment wealth program, you will wake some Monday morning and find that you're not heading off to the office or factory. And that's great. But what then? Okay, you're going to have an extra cup of coffee and leisurely read the morning paper. And then what? Maybe you've got a special project that'll take you a day, a week, or even a month. But then what? You see my point. This book talks about how to prepare financially for the day you no longer have to work. But you and I need to prepare in other ways, too. And this preparation is just as important, perhaps even more important.

To be totally honest with you—and here I'm just speaking as a friend, not an expert—I think you've got, I've got, a handful of choices:

- Undertake some new work experience or adventure. Now, people with jobs they don't like scoff at this. But I think it's a compelling option. Why not get some new, interesting job? Maybe you can be a European tour guide. Or play drums in some jazz band. When you don't have to consider the money part of some job opportunity, when you can quit if the work doesn't pan out, well, that makes things different.

- Find a hobby or activity. This is a traditional retirement notion. People spend time doing hobbies they never had enough time for when they worked: golf, fishing, square dancing, or whatever. I think the hobby angle is a fine one. But my observations have been that you want to develop mature interests before that first Monday morning of financial independence. I've also noted—and you've probably seen the same thing—that most people can't spend five days a week on some hobby.

- Begin a mission. Maybe you can do something to make the world a better or safer place. For example, what if you spend time teaching disadvantaged kids how to read? Or maybe working for responsible economic development in some poor country? Or maybe helping clean up your neighborhood or community? I found myself particularly intrigued by this notion, by the idea of volunteering my energy and time for some meaningful charity. I'm not sure exactly what I would do. But one sees people make real contributions after they've reached financial independence and decided they no longer want to work. You might want to do this, too.

HAVE YOUR WILL WRITTEN OR UPDATED

A will tells the state how you want your assets distributed when you die. If you have children, it also tells the state who you want to take care of your children.

While most people know they need a will, what people often don't know is that there are two reasons one needs a will. First and most obvious is that if you don't have a will that specifies how your assets should be distributed and where your kids should go, the state decides this stuff for you. Unfortunately, what the state decides may be the exact opposite of what you want to happen. Your money may all go to some good-for-nothing relative. Your kids may end up living with some well-meaning but totally incapable in-law.

But there's also a second reason why people—particularly people who've begun to accumulate a bit of money—should have a will drawn up. If your total net worth exceeds a set amount—$625,000 at the time I'm writing this, although this amount will rise to $1,000,000 over the next few years—estate taxes may take a huge bite out of your estate and leave only the remainder for your heirs. Chapter 8 talks about this in more detail in answering the question "Will an investment wealth program make my kids rich?"

With a well-written will and some advance planning, however, an attorney can in many cases eliminate the need to pay estate taxes. Note that this sort of estate planning work isn't expensive, either. You're probably talking as little as a few hundred dollars and certainly not more than a couple of thousand dollars. You'll probably pay at the low end of that range if you live in a small town or city and at the high end of the range if you live in a large city or work with a big law firm.

Let me make one other, quick comment about having a will drawn up. When you do this, I'd suggest you take the time to review your investment wealth program with your attorney. You don't have to say that you're trying to get rich. And, in fact, you probably shouldn't. But mention that you're seriously and aggressively putting away money into a

401(k) plan or IRA or whatever. And then ask your attorney if there are any asset protection measures you should consider or implement. In other words, is there anything you should or can do to protect your growing investment portfolio and even your other property against the claims of government agencies, creditors, and litigants?

What your attorney will probably say is that you're in good shape because of your insurance—especially the personal liability umbrella policy you read about in Chapter 5—and because money in retirement accounts like 401(k) plans and IRAs is generally unavailable to creditors. This is true in most although not all states. And that's fine. But you do want to check this stuff. As you become more and more wealthy, you will become a bigger financial target. And it's possible that your attorney, knowing the specifics of your situation, may counsel you to use one or more asset protection or estate planning tactics.

My attorney explains it to people this way: "When you're rich, people view you as a money tree. What they figure—and they're right—is that it usually makes sense to shake a money tree. Almost always at least a little money falls out. . . ."

HAVE A PERSONAL FINANCIAL PLAN WRITTEN

What the Millionaire Kit describes, plain and simple, is how you accumulate wealth. And that's an important part of any personal financial plan because it means, among other things, that you can retire. But there's more to personal financial planning than simply getting rich.

Several other personal financial planning tasks loom on your horizon. If you're in the final decade of a career—and perhaps even sooner—you probably want to restructure your portfolio so you can count on a regular stream of income. Chapter 8 talks about the basic way you do this in the answer to the question "Why shouldn't someone invest in bonds?"

If you're about to retire, you may have other questions or concerns, too, such as about Social Security or pension benefits, medical insurance, and even Medicare.

These other issues are important, and you need to think about them beforehand. For this reason, I strongly urge you to have a personal financial plan drawn up at some point in the future. You probably don't need to do it right away. If you've got kids who may attend college, you *do* need to begin saving money for their college expenses right away, as I discuss a bit later in this chapter.

But at some point—maybe a decade or so before you plan to retire—what you want to do is sit down and talk with someone about how you can restructure your investment portfolio so it produces consistent, dependable income at the point that you reach financial independence. You might do this by moving money from stock mutual funds to bonds, for example. And you probably also want to get some expert advice concerning any of the decisions you'll ultimately need to make about how you receive your pension and any other retirement benefits. Sometimes you need to decide whether a pension benefit is based on just your life expectancy or both you and your spouse's life expectancies.

If you've run a successful investment program, you are not going to encounter any big problems. But there are a bunch of decisions you'll need to make as you step into financial independence. And you'll richly benefit by getting some timely, professional, unbiased advice.

You can consult a variety of people for personal financial planning help. And the most useful bit of advice that I can give you is to find someone who's trustworthy and competent. To do this, you probably need to ask friends and people like your attorney, your certified public accountant, and your banker for recommendations. If you keep hearing one name over and over, or you get a recommendation from someone whom you can trust, you've probably found your personal financial planner.

I recommend that you work with either an estate planning attorney who also does personal financial planning work or a certified public accountant who does personal financial planning and possesses the Personal

Financial Specialist, or PFS, designation. I believe you're more likely to get somebody really smart and really good in this way.

I discourage you from attempting to use someone who's essentially a commissioned salesperson such as an insurance agent, stockbroker, or investment sales agent, for personal planning advice. And I'm personally leery of personal financial planners who earn all of their income from sales commissions on the products they sell. There are some excellent personal financial planners who earn sales commissions, I grant you that. But if you get a mediocre commissioned salesperson dispensing advice, there's often a real risk that this advisor's suggestions are influenced by the commissions he or she will receive.

What's more, at the point that you've become wealthy and have perhaps hundreds of thousands of dollars of financial assets, you don't want to pay for personal financial advice by paying sales commissions. You'll pay way, way too much for the advice. For example, at the point you've accumulated, say, $250,000 in your investment portfolio, the last thing you want to do is pay a $25,000 sales commission. That makes sense, right? And yet, if you go to some personal financial planner who gets paid via sales commission, that's exactly what may happen. In comparison, you can probably sit down for half a day with a world-class attorney or certified public accountant and pay $1,000 or less.

All this said, let me say again that the most important thing is for you to have someone who's trustworthy and smart. A trustworthy and smart personal financial planner—even one who is paid via sales commissions— is a better deal than some attorney or certified public accountant who isn't trustworthy or isn't smart.

One final quick point: If you do use a personal financial planner who is paid via commission, I think you should ask this person upfront to disclose the sales commissions he or she will receive if you purchase any of the products he or she sells. You can tell him or her that you read you're supposed to do this in this book.

PERIODICALLY RECALCULATE YOUR WEALTH ACCUMULATION PLAN

Every so often—maybe at the end of the year—you should recalculate the amount you should be saving each month. This point makes intuitive sense, right? If you've maybe underestimated inflation or overestimated the annual return, you want a chance to correct your forecasting error. Another thing is that over time you might change your definition of financial independence, deciding that you want more or less money than you've thought in the past. To recalculate your investment wealth program, use the Financial Independence Calculator introduced in Chapter 1.

Let me point out a related factor here, too. As your income changes, your definition of financial independence will and should change. For example, if you're making $20,000 a year, you may view financial independence as requiring $20,000 a year in investment portfolio income. If your income grows to $40,000 a year, you may update your definition of financial independence, viewing independence as requiring $30,000 a year or perhaps more. Similarly, if your income drops, your definition may also change.

Adjusting your definition of financial independence isn't bad, by the way. It reflects financial balance. When you boil down an investment wealth program to its very essence, all you're really doing is arranging your finances in such a way that with the help of compound interest you use, say, thirty years of earnings to pay for fifty or sixty years of living. This makes sense, right? If you work from age twenty-five to age fifty-five and then enjoy financial independence from age fifty-five to age eighty-five, you've actually used thirty years (from age twenty-five to age fifty-five) of earnings plus compound interest to support sixty years of living (from age twenty-five to age eighty-five).

What's more, if you do adjust your definition of financial independence for changes in your income, you'll find that your consumption and lifestyle changes less than your income. If your income shoots up, for example, you'll find the need to rather dramatically increase your savings if you adjust your definition of financial independence upward. And if your income drops off and you adjust your definition downward, you'll find it possible to reduce—and sometimes even eliminate—your need to continue contributing to your savings. Another way to say this same thing is that by adjusting your definition of financial independence, you can dampen the volatility of swings in your income. And that's really good.

CONSIDER EARLY RETIREMENT

Let me say one more thing that's tangentially related to the investment wealth program described in this book. While most people think you need to be age fifty-nine and a half to begin withdrawing money from a retirement account without paying a 10 percent early withdrawal penalty, there are actually several circumstances under which you can begin withdrawing money from a tax-deferred, tax-deductible retirement account before age fifty-nine and a half without penalty. You can begin withdrawing money if you become disabled from injury or illness and can no longer work, for example. You can begin withdrawing retirement investment savings if you stop working after age fifty-five. And, most interestingly, you can also generally withdraw the money early if you take the money in an annuity. An annuity is just an equal stream of payments.

That you can withdraw money from your retirement accounts as an annuity means you can retire whenever you want to retire, assuming you have the funds. For example, if you accumulate a large enough portfolio that you want to retire at age forty-five, you can probably withdraw money from your IRA, 401(k), or SEP at that point.

In setting up a stream of payments, or annuity, you'll want to get the help of a personal financial planner to make sure that what I've said here still applies when you're ready to begin taking the money. What's more, it's possible that there are more desirable ways to structure the annuity in your situation. If this is the case, you'll benefit from the expert advice.

DON'T PLAY WITH YOUR MONEY

As tempting as it will become, do resist the urge to play with your money once you become wealthy. Now that sounds terrible. So let me explain.

You don't want to make the mistake of turning your investments into a hobby. Yet, in my observations, wealthy people frequently do turn their money into a hobby and almost always with disastrous result. They buy investments like commodities or shares in newly public companies with risks they don't understand. They lend money to people who aren't creditworthy, such as kids trying to start businesses. And then they spend more money paying for newsletters, tax advice, and financial counseling than the extra profits they can ever hope to make.

I have no way of gauging whether you can truly afford a racehorse or sailboat once you complete your investment wealth program. But even so, I suggest you'll find either of these hobbies less expensive, ultimately, than playing with your money. At least with a racehorse or a sailboat, you'll be more apt to recognize your hobby expenses as just that. You probably won't foul up your financial independence—or at least not without realizing it. And you'll be much less likely to someday leave a financial mess for your spouse or heirs.

DON'T FORGET YOUR KIDS' COLLEGE COSTS

The investment wealth program that this book describes almost certainly means that you don't need to worry about retirement planning. If you've accumulated enough money that you don't have to work, obviously, you don't need to worry about how to survive financially during retirement. Although as mentioned earlier, you will need to restructure your investment portfolio before you retire so that your portfolio produces a safe and steady stream of income.

There is, however, one other big financial management task that you need to consider, so I'll mention it here: your kids' college costs. As you undoubtedly know, sending your kids to college costs a small fortune. And unless you want to borrow or want your kids to borrow the money for college—and thereby end college in debt up to their eyeballs—you'll want to save some money beforehand or prepare yourself to pay significant college costs out of pocket. This isn't a book about paying for college, but nevertheless, I can quickly give you some pretty useful advice and information. There are several things you should know.

First, there really isn't much true financial aid available. Most of the money that people call "financial aid" is really just a bunch of loans. In other words, there is no free money—except in a small handful of cases for the very poorest families or the very brightest kids. For most students, one way or another, either you or the student ends up paying for college. You've generally got three choices as to when and how you pay: You can pay for college beforehand by saving money early. You can pay for college as a child is in school. And you can pay for college after the fact by getting so-called financial aid loans.

If you're going to pay for college ahead of time—by saving money early—you can use the same process as the one you use for saving money for an investment wealth program. By periodically putting away a bit of money into an investment account, you may be able to save quite a bit of money over any reasonable length of time.

You have two options as to how you do this. The most obvious option is that you invest the money in the same manner that you invest your regular investment portfolio. The problem with this approach, however, is that you're typically investing money for a much shorter time period when you're talking about college than when you're talking about financial independence. So you probably shouldn't invest heavily in the stock market unless you begin saving when your son or daughter or grandson or granddaughter is born or even before. If your child is still in diapers or at least preschool, for example, put part of your money in stocks and then put the rest of your money in bonds or an intermediate-term bond mutual fund. You want to do this just in case the stock market does poorly between now and the time your young scholar enters college.

To reduce your risks, I recommend you invest the first half of your money in the stock market and use this money for the last half of college, and then put the second half of your money in bonds and use this money for the first half of college. This sounds unnecessarily complex, but let me explain why I make this suggestion. Say your child is four years old and that it will be fourteen years until he graduates from high school. In this case, you put your first seven years of savings into the stock market and then use this money for the student's junior and senior years of college. And then put the second seven years of savings into the bond market and use this money for the student's freshman and sophomore years of college. In this way, you'll be able to stretch out the length of your stock market investment to almost twenty years, and thereby reduce your risk.

Insight

Use the COLLEGE SAVINGS CALCULATOR from the companion CD to estimate how much money you should save on a monthly basis in order to pay for a child's college expenses or some portion of those expenses out of savings rather than through student loans. To do so, follow these steps:

STEP 1   Start the College Savings Calculator in the same manner as you start any Windows or Macintosh program.

STEP 2   Enter the college expenses you want to pay from savings into the **Annual college costs you will pay with savings** box.

STEP 3   Enter the time it will take your young scholar to complete college into the **Years of college** box.

STEP 4   Enter the number of years you have to save before your child starts college into the **Years until college** box.

Insight (continued)

STEP 5   Enter the amount you've already saved for college into the **Money you've already saved** box. If you haven't yet saved anything, enter 0 into this box.

STEP 6   Enter an estimate of the inflation rate you expect over the years you'll save and the years your child will attend college into the **Inflation rate you expect** box. Note that in recent years, college costs have inflated at a rate that exceeds the general inflation rate.

STEP 7   Enter an estimate of the interest rate you'll earn on your investments into the **Annual interest rate** box. For example, if you think you'll earn 8 percent, enter 8.

STEP 8   Use the **Will you save through college** option buttons to indicate whether you want to continue saving as your child attends college (mark **Yes** in this case) or whether you want to finish saving before your child enters college (mark **No** in this case).

STEP 9   Click the **Estimate** button, and the College Savings Calculator estimates the amount you must save each month in order to pay your child's college costs. It's a good idea to recheck this calculation every year to make sure that you're still on track with your college savings plan.

STEP 10   Optionally, click the **Print** button to print a permanent copy of your calculation results.

Let me make three additional and very quick observations about where and how you should store any college savings money. First of all, while some people tell you to use retirement vehicles like your 401(k) account or an IRA, I recommend that you *not* do this. Okay, it's true that retirement savings typically aren't included in financial aid calculations. And it's also true that the tax savings you accrue usually more than make up for any early withdrawal penalty. But here's my perspective in this matter: I don't think you want to muck about with your tax-deductible, tax-deferred investment options for the sake of college savings. You need to use your retirement savings accounts, such as 401(k)s and IRAs, for your investment wealth program. And if you start using them for college savings, what you gain in the way of extra money for college you more than lose when you consider the effect on your investment wealth program.

That sounds cruel at first. But I don't think it is. Sure. Using retirement savings accounts does help you save money for your kids' college because of the income tax savings. But it can also easily screw up your investment wealth program. Let's say you need to save $4,000 a year for your investment wealth program and $4,000 for college and that your only tax-deductible investment option is a $4,000 IRA. If you use the IRA for your college savings money, then you can't use it for retirement. And that means that you're not on track to financial independence.

One other thing about this college savings business: You probably want to give some consideration as to the name in which the college savings are invested. If you invest the money in your kid's name, you get a slight income tax benefit—which is good—but then the savings reduce the amount of financial aid available. What's more, if the money is in your kid's name, when your son or daughter reaches your state's age of majority—probably either eighteen or twenty-one—your child can do whatever he or she wants with the money. Go to Europe. Get married. Buy a sports car, or whatever. If you trust your kids and will save most of the money you need for college anyway, I think the tax benefit of putting money in your child's name is worth the risk that your kids will go off and blow the money on something stupid. I do this with my kids, by the way. But you'll need to analyze how this trade-off—tax savings versus less financial aid and the risks of immaturity—works in your family.

If you're uncomfortable with using the stock market for college savings money—and quite frankly the stock market doesn't work as well for college as it does for financial independence—you can also try another approach. What you can do is prepay your mortgage so that you make your last mortgage payment before your child enters college. Then, when your son or daughter enters college, you can redirect the amount you have been paying toward your mortgage to college tuition bills. This isn't a perfect method because you don't know for sure whether or not your annual mortgage payments will pay for a child's full college bill—or two children's full college bills. But let's say you've been paying off a $100,000 mortgage over fifteen years with roughly $1,000-a-month payments. If you stop making these payments the year before your child enters school, you should have enough money to pay for a year of college. And with a little bit of jiggling, many families could put a couple of children through school using this method. If any financial aid loans were required, these amounts could probably be quickly paid in the year or two following graduation by just continuing to redirect the old mortgage payment amount to repay the student loan.

Insight

Use the LOAN CALCULATOR from the companion CD to calculate what size loan payment you need to make in order to have your mortgage paid off by the time your child enters college. To do so, follow these steps:

STEP 1   Start the Loan Calculator in the same manner as you start any Windows or Macintosh program.

STEP 2   Mark the **Regular payment** option button. (The **Regular payment** button is part of the **Loan variable to calculate** set of option buttons.)

STEP 3   Mark the **monthly** option button. (The **monthly** button is part of the **Payment made every** set of option buttons.)

STEP 4   Enter the current loan balance into the **Loan balance** box.

Insight (continued)

STEP 5   Enter the number of years until your child enters college into the **Repayment term** box. For example, if your child is eight and will enter college in ten years at age eighteen, enter 10.

STEP 6   Enter the loan's annual interest rate into the **Annual interest rate** box. For example, if you think you'll earn 8.375 percent, enter 8.375.

STEP 7   Enter 0 into the **Balloon payment** box.

STEP 8   Click the **Estimate** button, and the Loan Calculator estimates the amount you must pay each month in interest and principal in order to repay your mortgage loan in full before your child enters college.

STEP 9   Optionally, click the **Print** button to print a permanent copy of your calculation results.

Chapter

8

COMMON QUESTIONS

One of the disadvantages of a book is that you can't sit down with the author, perhaps over a cup of coffee, and ask questions about the material you've read or reviewed. And that's unfortunate. It's easy for the author to omit coverage of some topic you're particularly interested in. Then, other times, the author will say something you don't quite understand. Or maybe you have unique interests. And in all these cases, it's nice to be able to ask a question.

I can't really answer all your questions in a chapter like this, of course. But what I'm going to try and do is answer a bunch of the most common or predictable questions that you and other readers might have. Hopefully, you'll get answers to your most important questions in this manner.

IS THE MILLIONAIRE KIT FORMULA A SURE THING?

No, it isn't. Because nothing is a sure thing.

But that said, I think it's as close to a sure thing as you can practically get. If you had run an investment wealth program over any twenty-five-year time period in the last hundred years in the United States, for example, the Millionaire Kit formula would have worked for you. For example, if you had started an investment wealth program in 1926 just before the great stock market crash but then stayed in the market through the Great

Depression of the 1930s and through World War II and into the early 1950s, the Millionaire Kit formula would have worked. Even over this tumultuous time period, the U.S. stock market delivered annual returns of just over 8 percent while the inflation rate hovered right around 2 percent. This meant that the real, or adjusted for inflation, rate of return equaled 6 percent, which is enough to run an investment wealth program.

Nevertheless, I should tell you that there are circumstances, even in recent history, where stock market investments would not have paid off—and in fact, would have proved disastrous. And because the Millionaire Kit formula depends on high real rates of returns, like those generated by stock markets, this means that in these circumstances the Millionaire Kit formula wouldn't always work.

If you had invested in the German stock market for a twenty-five-year time frame starting in the 1920s, for example, an investment wealth program would not have worked. After the Great Depression, the Nazi rise to power, and World War II, your German holdings probably would have no value by the end of the war. Similarly, if you had invested in the stock market in any of the Eastern European countries in the old communist bloc prior to the rise of communism, the value of your holdings would have dropped to zero when the government nationalized whole industries. In even more recent history, you might easily lose all your money investing in the stock markets of emerging nations, perhaps because of political or economic instability. So in these special circumstances, stocks aren't a good investment. And, as a result, the Millionaire Kit formula wouldn't work.

Yet, my position is that you can't and shouldn't let these examples dissuade you from running an investment wealth program. For one thing, you can diversify away many of the worst investment risks simply by holding a wide range of stocks or by investing principally in the world's major economies—the United States, Japan, and Germany—which are all now democratic, free market economy countries.

The other thing is that if you start looking at worst-case scenarios, I'm not sure what that leaves you with. Bonds aren't going to do any better in a worst-case scenario. Neither is real estate. Interestingly, real estate property insurance policies—including your homeowners policy—explicitly exclude acts of war from coverage. I suppose you can hoard gold or diamonds or some other extremely precious and relatively portable commodity. But even that doesn't really work—at least when you consider the big picture. In some ways, if you've got a situation that's as dangerous or unstable as, say, Nazi Germany was, gold doesn't help you. Many of the things that threaten the returns of financial investments may also threaten your personal safety and physical security. It strikes me as grim irony, for example, that in the early days of Nazi Germany, many German Jews apparently deposited gold into Swiss bank accounts looking for safety—money that, at least at this writing, Holocaust victims' heirs have been largely unsuccessful in claiming.

So, to sum things up, the Millionaire Kit formula isn't a sure thing. But with a little luck, it's almost a sure thing. And as I've repeatedly said through the pages of this book, if you can get the money you need to run an investment wealth program from the government or from your employer, and by making a smarter decision or two, how can you not do this?

HOW DOES THE MILLIONAIRE KIT FORMULA RELATE TO VOLUNTARY SIMPLICITY?

Voluntary simplicity, as you may know, refers to the philosophy of joyfully living with less. For example, people who adopt voluntary simplicity typically find or create economical housing—often sharing a house or apartment with other people. These people also learn to stretch their dollars to incredible lengths by recycling and reusing everything from clothing to coffee. Sometimes people also combine a philosophy of voluntary simplicity with an aggressive savings program that means they're saving 20 percent, 30 percent, or even more of their income. On the face of it, then, voluntary simplicity can look like the Millionaire Kit formula.

But the Millionaire Kit formula doesn't require voluntary simplicity. Sure, voluntary simplicity is compatible with the Millionaire Kit. In fact, you could combine the two strategies and reach financial independence in a few years. But here's the deal: The Millionaire Kit formula assumes you find the money you need to run an investment wealth program by making one or two or three big but rather clever decisions. Voluntary simplicity, in comparison, often requires or suggests that you make dozens and perhaps even hundreds of sacrifices and decisions—some big and some small.

WHY SHOULDN'T SOMEONE INVEST IN BONDS?

If you read any of the investment literature, you'll repeatedly come across this idea that you should invest part of your investment portfolio in stocks and then part in bonds. The justification for this is that if the stock market doesn't perform well some years, you'll still get a decent return on your bonds.

If you look at the year-to-year returns of stocks and bonds over any reasonable time—like over the last couple of decades—this argument seems pretty solid. You'll have bad years in the stock market. And I totally agree with this. But with bonds, at least you can be assured of making a little bit of money. And I totally agree with this, too.

What's more, over long periods of time, by holding a portion of your investments in bonds, you suffer only a modest drop in the rate of return delivered by your portfolio while dramatically reducing its volatility. Since the stock market crash of 1929, for example, an investment portfolio made up of 60 percent stocks and 40 percent bonds would have produced annual average returns of just under 9 percent. An investment portfolio made up of all stocks would have produced annual average returns of just over 10 percent. So, bonds can seem good. And you'll be in good company if you decide to put 20 percent or even 40 percent of your investment money into bonds or a bond mutual fund. But I don't like bonds for people who are beginning thirty-year or forty-year investment wealth programs.

There are several practical problems with employing bonds in an investment wealth program. The first and biggest problem is this: They don't deliver a return high enough to provide significant compound interest, after you adjust for inflation. For example, if you invest $2,000 a year in an inflation-indexed U.S. Treasury bond, you'll earn slightly over 3 percent and accumulate around $130,000 after thirty-five years. That sounds pretty good, but remember that $70,000 of that sum is really just money you've saved anyway. So, in this case, you really only make about $60,000 of interest. In comparison, if you invest $2,000 a year in the stock market and earn, say, a 6.5 percent real rate of return, you accumulate right around $250,000 dollars. And in this case, you make about $180,000 of interest.

Think about those numbers for a minute. In one case you make $60,000, and in the other you make $180,000. That's the first problem in a nutshell: Over any extended period of time, you just can't make all that much money once you adjust for inflation if you use bonds. With stocks you can.

Here's a second problem of using bonds in an investment wealth program. There is no twenty-five-year or thirty-five-year time frame in the recent past when you would have done better by owning a diversified portfolio of bonds than you would have by owning a diversified portfolio of stocks. And this makes sense. If bonds consistently produced better overall returns than stocks, it would mean that people preferred to invest in riskier stock investments and, therefore, were happier earning a risky 3 percent stock investment return in place of a riskless 6 percent bond investment return.

People aren't stupid. They will always require a bit of extra return for the uncertainty of stock ownership. And that means to me that over the long term, stocks must outperform bonds.

As part of a long-term investment wealth program, therefore, I don't think bonds make sense. I agree they reduce your financial risk because they make your returns more predictable. But they just don't produce enough interest to work in an investment wealth program.

Okay, now all of that said, you probably will use bonds in two special circumstances. First of all, bonds make good sense for your rainy-day fund. If you've accumulated a substantial sum of money in your rainy-day fund, you might want to invest the money in a short-term bond fund. If you're a risktaker with a stable, strong income, you might even want to invest the money in an intermediate-term bond fund. In either of these cases, you'll probably earn more in interest in the bond fund than you will in a money market fund or bank savings account. The longer the average maturity of the bonds in a bond fund, the more the bond fund share price bounces around as interest rates fluctuate, and that's not good, of course. However, longer maturity bonds also typically pay higher interest rates.

If you're a high-income taxpayer, you may even want to use a municipal bond fund or money market fund, since these bonds often pay interest that is tax-exempt. Note, by the way, that if you follow the advice given in Chapter 5 about building a sizable rainy-day fund, you will probably have in excess of 10 percent of your investment wealth allocated to bonds in the first few years of your investment wealth program.

A second thing to note is that as you approach retirement, you'll want to move a large chunk of your investment portfolio from stocks to bonds. The reason for this is simple: At the point you achieve financial independence, you'll find stable, predictable income more important than additional wealth. And bonds do provide stable income. For example, let's say you want to have $60,000 of retirement income that you can count on every year. If you can invest in $1,000,000 of bonds that pay 6 percent and you can depend on the borrower, you know that no matter what you'll get your $60,000 of retirement income. If the stock market crashes, you'll still make $60,000. If there's war in the Middle East, you'll still make your $60,000. If some rogue country detonates a thermonuclear device, you'll still make your $60,000.

So what a lot of people do—and I'll probably do this in the years before I quit working—is build a portfolio of bonds that pay predictable, steady, dependable interest income. In other words, I may take, say, $1,000,000 out of the stock market where it may be earning $90,000 or even $100,000 a year and invest it into bonds that pay $60,000 a year.

Since we're on the subject, let me also mention that the way I'll probably do this is by moving, for example, $100,000 or $200,000 a year out of the stock market and into ten-year U.S. Treasury bonds. Ten years before I quit working, I'll take $100,000 or $200,000 out of the market and use this money to buy ten-year U.S. Treasury bonds. A year later, I'll do the same thing again. And then I'll do the same thing a few more times until I have $1,000,000 in bonds producing predictable, steady income. This process, by the way, is called building a bond ladder, and it's a way to create a stream of very safe, very steady income.

I mentioned this in the last chapter, but one of the reasons why you want to have a personal financial plan done—say a decade before you retire—is so that you can intelligently restructure your portfolio so it emphasizes income rather than growth.

WHY CAN'T SOMEONE INVEST DIRECTLY IN REAL ESTATE?

A lot of people are excited about direct real estate investment because it lets you use financial leverage—therefore amplifying your profits—and because everybody seems to know at least one person who's made a lot of money in real estate.

The problem with real estate—and I mentioned this in Chapter 2—is that it probably doesn't on average produce better returns than the stock market. And yet it suffers from several disadvantages. You can't easily diversify with real estate. Owning half a dozen rental houses in your hometown doesn't represent diversification, for example. And real estate is also usually illiquid. If you need to buy or sell a particular property, it'll take weeks, months, and maybe even years. One other problem with direct real estate investment is that you can't directly invest in real estate and get the same tax-deduction and tax-deferral benefits that come with options like IRAs and 401(k)s.

You can purchase shares in equity real estate investment trusts, or equity REITs, and in mutual funds that invest in equity real estate investment trusts if you really want to hold a portion of your investment portfolio in real estate. Equity REITs own real estate: hotels, apartment houses, office buildings, industrial parks, and so forth.

WHY NOT TRY INVESTING DIRECTLY IN THE STOCK MARKET?

You can do this. And you probably can reduce your annual investment expenses if you've accumulated a lot of money already. But the main thing is, you want to make sure that you've got enough individual stocks that you know your returns will average out to the stock market average. This probably means that you need at least a dozen stocks in a wide variety of industries.

All this said, what most people will find is that large, low-cost mutual funds—particularly index mutual funds—work best. Sure. You may be able to eke out a small improvement in your annual return by directly investing in stocks. But you can hardly beat the convenience of mutual funds.

WHY NOT TRY TO PICK HOT MUTUAL FUNDS AND BEAT THE AVERAGES?

Some newspapers and numerous magazines promote this idea—the notion that you can and should pick hot mutual funds, thereby beating the average. It's an appealing idea. Why not beat the market? Why settle for average returns?

Nevertheless, I think this notion is extremely suspect. First of all, if some magazine or newsletter editor or writer is so clever that he or she knows which mutual funds will outperform the market, this person shouldn't be writing magazine articles for $1 a word or editing magazine articles for $30 an hour. No way. He or she should be running an investment advisory firm. The average mutual fund manager, by the way, makes around $300,000 a year, which is a lot more than the average magazine editor makes.

You can laugh about me saying this. But think about it. If people really know which mutual funds or stocks or bonds will outperform the market, they should be able to convert that knowledge into millions of dollars of income a year. Right?

A second, more objective thing to consider is that no academic study has ever shown—and finance professors look at this stuff all the time—that mutual fund recommendations enable people to substantially beat the market. In fact, the opposite is true because of the way that many of these magazines and newsletters often pick their favorites. What these magazines and newsletters tend to do is pick mutual funds that have recently outperformed the market. The assumption is that the good times will continue. But these high-rolling mutual funds often aren't the ones that continue to outperform the market. After a period where they outperform the market, they tend to under-perform the market. And, actually, this makes sense if you consider the statistical truism that over the long haul, things tend to average out to the average. This tendency is so often observed, by the way, that statisticians have even given a name to it: regression to the mean.

So, I don't think this is a good tactic. It makes far more sense just to lock in the average or close to the average return. You can and will get rich if you earn the stock market's average return.

WHAT IF THE STOCK MARKET CRASHES?

As I'm writing this in early 1998, the stock market seems overvalued to me. It therefore seems very possible that either as this book is published or shortly after it's published, we will see a major unfavorable change in the stock market's values. Yet even so, I don't believe that a stock market crash needs to matter to someone who is just beginning an investment wealth program.

But let me explain why by providing a concrete example. Let's say that in your investment wealth program you plan to save $10,000 a year for twenty-five years in order to amass a $1,000,000 investment portfolio. Let's also say that the stock market crashes by 50 percent the year after you begin your investment wealth program. If things really did work out this way, I suspect many investors would, well, basically freak out. But I don't think you should for two reasons.

First of all, if the stock market does lose 50 percent of its value in the year after you begin your investment wealth program, you will lose half your money. A year after you've begun your journey to financial independence, half your money equals roughly $5,000. But while $5,000 seems like a lot of money—and I guess it is—$5,000 is not very much compared to the $250,000 you will contribute over the twenty-five years that you run your investment wealth program. And $5,000 is not very much compared to the $750,000 of compound interest you'll probably earn over the twenty-five years. And most important, $5,000 is not very much compared to the ultimate $1,000,000 investment portfolio you will amass.

You need to keep this big-picture perspective and these big numbers in your mind. Yes, a $5,000 loss as you're just starting out is huge. And my guess is you really will suffer a large, early loss like this. But because you're using dollar-cost averaging in your investing as discussed in Chapter 2 and because you will have years and years over which to recover from any crash, your real risk is not all that great. And that's the first and most important thing to understand about a stock market crash.

Now here's the second thing you should know. Financial research suggests that after a period of above-average stock market returns, like the period that we've had over the last fifteen years, investors comfortably bear more risk and accept lower returns. This same research also suggests that after a period of below-average stock market returns, investors only uncomfortably bear risk and demand higher returns. You can apply this theory in a variety of ways, but note that if we do have a big crash, the crash itself may produce an environment that's very favorable to people like you who are running long-term investment wealth programs. In other words, if there is any environment in which you might be able to earn above average rates of return, it's probably one where scared investors are demanding higher returns because of a recent stock market crash.

Okay, I want to say one last thing to you about a stock market crash. While a big stock market crash—like the 50 percent crash described earlier—shouldn't scare people just starting their investment wealth programs, such a crash does matter to people finishing their investment wealth programs. A few paragraphs ago, for example, I introduced the example where someone is saving $10,000 a year in order to amass $1,000,000. In this situation, a 50 percent stock market crash doesn't have to foul up a person just starting their investment wealth program. But a 50 percent stock market crash at the finish line of such an investment wealth program—when the person in our example has accumulated $1,000,000— means a $500,000 loss. And that is a killer. With a 50 percent loss just before the finish line, a person can't recover from the loss by contributing another payment or two to their investment portfolio. And a person can't expect the investment portfolio to earn its way out of the $500,000 hole in any short-term period of time. Going from $500,000 to $1,000,000 in value by earning normal rates of return, for example, could easily take a decade or more.

I mention this prospect not to scare you. But only to point out once again that as you get closer to financial independence—say when you're a decade away or so—you'll want to begin restructuring your portfolio so that it emphasizes income rather than growth. This restructuring isn't difficult. And it's not something you need to worry about right away. But dog-ear this chapter of this book. And then several years before you reach financial independence, either take the time to have a personal financial plan written as discussed in the last chapter, or read the most up-to-date article you can find on building a bond ladder. Note that I did describe in general terms how you build a bond ladder in answer to the question, "Why shouldn't someone invest in bonds?"

HOW ABOUT ANNUITIES?

Annuities, which are sold by insurance companies, aren't bad. In general, annuities let investors defer taxes on the income an annuity earned. And that's good. There are, however, a couple of problems with annuities. And you should know what they are.

First, contributions you make to an annuity aren't tax deductible. This means that tax-deductible, tax-deferred investment choices like 401(k)s and IRAs will always do better than an annuity. With both annuities and retirement accounts like 401(k)s and IRAs, you get tax deferral. Remember that tax deferral just means you don't have to pay taxes as your portfolio earns money; you pay taxes when you withdraw the money. But you only get the tax-deduction benefit with retirement accounts like 401(k)s and IRAs. As Chapter 2 points out, the tax deduction is important because it lets you effortlessly boost your savings simply by also contributing savings that any tax deductions generate.

A second thing to note is that insurance companies charge extra fees for annuities. You can end up paying a load, or commission, for an annuity, for example. And that obviously reduces your portfolio value at the very start. What's more, insurance companies also levy an extra annual fee on annuities. These extra charges make an annuity relatively less profitable.

In a situation where you have used up all of your tax-deductible, tax-deferred investment options like 401(k)s, where you can't invest additional money into regular IRAs or Roth IRAs, or when you've used up any other tax-deferred investment options like a nondeductible IRA, you might want to use an annuity. For example, say you and your spouse both work someplace where there's a 401(k) plan and that together you make $80,000. In this case, the two of you could probably collectively contribute $20,000 to the company's 401(k) plan. You would probably also be able to contribute another $4,000 to either a regular IRA or a Roth IRA. In the case where you also wanted to save another $10,000, you could do so, with tax advantages, by using an annuity.

In this case, what you probably want to look at first are no-load variable rate annuities such as those offered by the major mutual fund companies. In these cases, a mutual fund company essentially pays an insurance company an extra fee—perhaps 0.4 percent—so the insurer will call the investment an annuity. You won't get a tax deduction, of course. And you will pay slightly higher fees. But you will get tax deferral.

WHAT IF EVERYONE DID THIS—WOULD IT STILL WORK?

Well, probably not. But it's easy to let big absolute numbers seem like big relative numbers. So let's talk about this point for just a minute. Let's say that *The Millionaire Kit* sells as many copies as the very best-selling personal finance books—say it sells 2,500,000 copies. And say everybody who buys the book immediately goes out and applies the strategies and tools provided here. That might seem to be too much. You might think the party would be over because there are too many people investing in 401(k)s, IRAs, and stocks. But I don't think so. With roughly 250,000,000 people in the country, these numbers would mean that only one of out every hundred people are running an investment wealth program. In absolute numbers, then, 2,500,000 sounds big. But that's still only 1 percent of the population, which is actually a pretty small relative number.

If you take even a slightly more conservative view, both the absolute and relative numbers get much smaller. Say, for example, that 1,000,000 people buy this book, that only half of them read the book, and then that half of the readers apply the book's principles. In this case, you have 250,000 people running an investment wealth program, and the relative number is now very tiny. If 250,000 people out of a country with more than 250,000,000 inhabitants are running the program, only one in a thousand is doing this. It's interesting to note, by the way, that some of the best studies of the affluent suggest that there are about a million millionaires in the country, which works out to roughly one millionaire for every 250 people.

So, to summarize, the investment wealth program this book describes doesn't stop working even if large, absolute numbers of people apply the program.

WHAT IF I JUST PLAIN CAN'T FIND THE MONEY?

Well, first of all, I think you can find the money. I'm not saying it's always easy or always painless. Although in most cases, finding the money is easy and is painless. But you should be able to find the money necessary to run an investment wealth program. Even if your income is very modest, it's very likely that there are people who make less than you do and still live a good life, right?

I don't want to keep beating this drum, but people with very modest incomes figure out how to pay for cigarettes. And just this money, if instead used for an investment wealth program, lets someone become a millionaire. The same thing applies to a bunch of bad habits, some of which I have and some of which you probably have, too.

What's more—and as I've said repeatedly through the pages of this book—you can probably get much and maybe even most of the money needed for your investment wealth program from your employer in the form of employer matching contributions and from the federal and state government in the form of income tax savings. And not only this, but as you begin to make smarter financial decisions using your computer, you will free up extra cash. If you use that extra cash for your investment wealth program, you will begin the journey toward financial independence. The main thing is, you need to start the journey. You need to get the compound interest engine as described in Chapter 2 working for you.

But all that said, let me share a final thought: If you really are having trouble coming up with the money for an investment wealth program, the easiest way to pump up your investment portfolio is by participating in a generous employer-sponsored retirement plan. In other words, find, join, or create an organization where your employer contributes money to your account. It's common in these plans for employers to contribute 2 percent to 3 percent of your salary. And that maybe doesn't seem like all that much money, but with these sorts of employer contributions, as noted elsewhere in this book, most of the money that goes into your investment portfolio comes from the federal and state government and from your employer. Remember, it's with these plans that you can turn $50 of your own money into, for example, a $150-a-month contribution. It's with these plans that you can turn $200 a month of your own money into a $600-a-month contribution.

Because employer contributions are so important—especially when you can't find the money anywhere else—you may want to do whatever needs to be done in order to participate in one of these plans. Maybe this means convincing your employer that something like a Simple-IRA or 401(k) is an important employee benefit. Or maybe this means you need to look for new employment. You need to think carefully about this, of course. But the point is that employer contributions go a long, long way toward providing the money you need.

WILL AN INVESTMENT WEALTH PROGRAM MAKE MY KIDS RICH?

Actually this is a really good question. So let's talk about it for just a minute. If you run through the numbers, it's pretty difficult for an individual to accumulate more than about a couple of million dollars using an investment wealth program like this book describes. What's more, most individuals will probably find it much easier to accumulate a million dollars in current-day, uninflated dollars. Note that the future-day numbers will actually be inflated and, therefore, larger.

But what this means is that even in the case of a married couple where both people work, the most money that one can practically accumulate is, maybe, $4,000,000: $2,000,000 in your retirement accounts and $2,000,000 in your spouse's retirement accounts. That's a lot of money, no doubt. But it's probably not enough to provide financial independence to your children because of the ways that income taxes and estate taxes work.

Does this surprise you? Let me explain. Say you and your spouse do accumulate $4,000,000 in your investment portfolios and that this amount generates $250,000 a year in investment income. In this case, it might seem as if you can share the wealth with your kids, but it's tougher than you think. If you two die tomorrow and your heirs roll the money out of this account in one big lump sum, for example, your estate and heirs will be hit with two rather large taxes. They will pay about a $1,200,000 federal estate tax bill. And then they will also pay federal income taxes of maybe $1,100,000. They may also pay state estate and income taxes. So, as kooky as it seems, therefore, your heirs might end up with less than half of the $4,000,000 you started with. If you then split this amount between your two kids, your kids end up with at most maybe $850,000 each and annual investment income of perhaps $50,000. Now obviously, this is a huge financial windfall for your heirs. But do note what's happened. In the best possible case where you have $4,000,000 in investment wealth and you annually earn perhaps $250,000 in investment income, your kids might easily end up with $850,000 each and maybe $50,000 a year of income. Sure. Your kids make out like bandits in this case. But their financial standing is radically different than yours.

Note, too, that most people aren't going to find themselves in the best case scenario. It's much more reasonable to figure you might end up with $1,000,000 in your investment portfolio. And while that $1,000,000 produces financial independence for you, when you take out the taxes and split the money, your heirs will be left with only a fraction of what you saved. With a $1,000,000 investment portfolio, you might pay around $130,000 in federal estate taxes, but your estate probably would pay close to $350,000 in federal income taxes.

Before you get discouraged about the difficulty of passing your wealth to the next generation, you should know that this inability to feather your children's nests probably isn't bad. Some pretty good studies have shown that kids who achieve financial independence via their parents' hard work don't actually end up in better shape. These kids tend to make not only less money but also poorer financial decisions. They get fat and lazy. And—this can be no surprise—they don't provide good role models for their children—your grandchildren—because the basic model they've demonstrated isn't one they can sustain. What your kids show their kids is that you just depend on your parents for financial help. Yet they'll never produce the wealth necessary to let their kids do the same thing.

Let me say one final thing about making your kids rich. If you really want to do this, the real trick is not to try to pass your wealth to your kids, which is tricky for the reasons described previously. The real trick is to get them started with an investment wealth program. For example, if at an early age you begin to stash money in tax-deductible, tax-deferred investment accounts and then you compound that money for forty or fifty years, you get truly amazing results. This sounds crazy, of course. But a lot of kids make hundreds of dollars a year—sometimes more—babysitting, mowing lawns, and delivering papers. If you want to help your kids achieve financial independence, you can give them a huge head start by plopping $500 a year or $1,000 a year or however much they earn into something like an IRA. If you do this for even a few years, your kids rather easily achieve multimillionaire status at age sixty-five.

By the way, because your kids don't get any income tax savings from using a regular deductible IRA, you want to use a Roth IRA for a child's or grandchild's investment wealth program. A Roth IRA doesn't provide an up-front tax deduction, but the later withdrawals are tax free. This is okay for a kid's investment wealth program, however. Kids typically don't get a tax deduction anyway because they don't make enough to pay any income taxes.

CAN YOU PUT TOO MUCH WEALTH INTO TAX-ADVANTAGED INVESTMENTS?

You sometimes hear people—even so-called financial experts—say that tax-deductible investment vehicles aren't all that good a deal because of the taxes you pay when you withdraw the money. You'll even sometimes hear people toss around percentages, saying things like, "Hey, you can lose 75 percent of the money you have in one of these accounts if you're not careful . . ." When you hear these sorts of comments—which contain grains of truth—it is unsettling. But it's not the problem that some people make it out to be.

Ultimately you may have to pay two separate taxes on the money in your account: income taxes and estate taxes. Let's begin by discussing the income taxes you'll pay.

When you pull money out of your IRA or 401(k), the government taxes you on the withdrawal. While that sounds unfair, remember what's really happened here. Your IRA or 401(k) account includes a bunch of money you should have originally paid in taxes. In effect, then, what's really happening is that the federal and state government just get back the money you originally should have paid in the form of income taxes each year.

Think of all this another way: If you put $10,000 into your 401(k), you probably ended up saving $3,000 in income taxes—and that's great. But when you pull the $10,000 out of your 401(k) a few years later, you will have to pay that $3,000. Therefore, someone who says you shouldn't put money into an IRA or a 401(k) because you'll someday have to pay income taxes on the withdrawal is wrong. What this person misses is that you're not paying any additional taxes. You're repaying the income taxes you originally saved. Yes, if you withdraw $10,000 from your 401(k), you might have to pay $3,000 in income taxes. But this is really just the same $3,000 you originally saved when you made the $10,000 contribution to the 401(k) in the first place. This little discussion also points out the essential economic benefit of tax-deductible investment vehicles: You borrow the money from the government for free, invest the money, and then keep all your profits.

The estate taxes issue is a bit more complicated, but here's a snapshot summary. Some people's estates are taxed at rates of up to 55 percent. Your estate pays any estate taxes after you die, so estate taxes really only affect your heirs. And if you are subject to estate tax, the money in your IRA or 401(k) will be taxed. As a result, some people mistakenly conclude that it can't make any sense to be accumulating wealth in an IRA or 401(k).

However, the estate tax situation isn't as bad as it first seems. You can pass your entire estate to your spouse without incurring any estate or income taxes, and similarly, your spouse can pass his or her entire estate to you without incurring any estate or income taxes. What's more, neither you nor your spouse actually pay estate taxes. You're dead when they come due, so estate taxes really only reduce the amount your heirs inherit. Finally, most heirs don't even get hit indirectly with estate taxes because in 1998, if you're single, your estate can pass $625,000 to your heirs without paying federal estate taxes. And this amount will rise over the next few years. By 2007, for example, you can pass $1,000,000 to your heirs without paying any federal estate taxes. If you are married and have a will drawn up by a smart attorney, your estate can probably pass double these amounts to your heirs without paying estate taxes: $1,250,000 in 1998 and then $2,000,000 in 2007. What's more, with just a little bit of up-front estate planning, you can easily move even more money out of your estate to your heirs without paying estate taxes.

Once you know all of this stuff, estate taxes don't have to scare you or your spouse. Consider the worst possible estate tax situation: You and your spouse accumulate as much money in an IRA or 401(k) as is practically possible, $4,000,000. In future inflated dollars, however, your portfolio will actually probably equal about $6,000,000. Let's also assume that you and your spouse die with this money untouched sometime after 2007. In this case, your estate and heirs will pay federal estate taxes of roughly $1,800,000. Your estate and heirs will also pay federal income taxes of roughly $1,700,000 which, as noted earlier, you would have had to pay anyway, leaving roughly $2,500,000 after the taxes.

If this retirement money is the only wealth your estate gets taxed on— and it can be with the help of a good estate tax attorney—your estate will end up paying around $1,800,000 in estate taxes. Which is a lot. But remember that this is the worst possible case. And while your heirs do get hit indirectly with a $1,800,000 estate tax bill, remember that they do inherit roughly $2,500,000 in future, inflated dollars. Okay, this amount would be worth less in current-day, uninflated dollars. But please note: We're completely ignoring the fact here that your heirs end up with a bigger jackpot because you ran a successful investment wealth program.

It's most likely that your situation won't be the worst possible case, of course. What if you end up with only slightly less money in your IRA or 401(k)—say you somehow have to make do on a *mere* $2,000,000? Or say that you don't die the day after you retire and so therefore spend some of your money? In these sorts of situations, your estate and heirs probably won't pay any federal estate taxes on your IRA or 401(k) money.

And let me just say this one last time: Remember that it's not you or your spouse paying the estate taxes. It's your estate and, therefore, really your heirs who end up paying estate taxes—and only if you've been just monstrously successful in your investment wealth program. You? You never have to pay the estate taxes.

The bottom line? Well, there are two things you should remember. First, tax-deductible investment vehicles don't require you to pay more in income taxes. Second, yes, your heirs may (indirectly) pay estate taxes—but that's really only because your investment wealth program is successful.

WHY HAVEN'T YOU TALKED ABOUT ROTH IRAS?

In 1997, Congress created several new types of IRAs, including one called a Roth IRA that can work in an investment wealth program. Roth IRAs are interesting. You don't get a tax deduction when you put money into one. But you also don't pay income taxes on your withdrawals. You do pay income taxes on the withdrawals from something like a 401(k) or a regular IRA.

While Roth IRAs seem intriguing, both 401(k)s and regular, deductible IRAs work better if you do the math and factor in the income taxes. A 401(k) plan works lots better because of the employer matching, which makes intuitive sense. And a deductible IRA works a little bit better than a Roth IRA because the tax deduction savings you get from making the contributions are worth more than the income savings you enjoy because the withdrawals are tax free. (This is so, by the way, because the marginal tax rate you use to figure the tax deduction from a deductible IRA is higher than the average tax rate you use to figure your tax savings from the Roth IRA.)

Your best bets, therefore, are things besides the Roth IRA. If you don't have other retirement savings choices available—such as a 401(k), a 403(b), or a deductible IRA—a Roth IRA works better than a nondeductible IRA or an annuity. For example, if your income is too high to qualify you for a regular deductible IRA, your next best choice would be a Roth IRA. This is because a different set of rules applies to Roth

IRAs—for one thing, your income can be a lot higher—so there may be reasons why some people want to use a Roth IRA. But most readers won't want to use a Roth IRA as part of an investment wealth program.

CAN I ACCELERATE MY INVESTMENT WEALTH PROGRAM?

As you know, this book describes a get-rich-slow scheme. The Millionaire Kit's basic idea is that you need to begin regularly saving and investing money, take advantage of tax-deductible and tax-deferred investment choices, and then bear the extra risk of the stock market to enjoy high, real rates of return.

But you presumably know all of this. And what you're really interested in is how you might accelerate the process. You may want to do in ten or twelve years what somebody else takes twenty-five years to do. So let's talk about this a bit.

You certainly can expedite things in little ways here and there. You can plow the maximum possible contributions into tax-deductible, tax-deferred investment options. If there's a 401(k) or 403(b) or Simple-IRA at work, you want to contribute the maximum amount. If you're married, your spouse also needs to make the maximum possible contribution.

Note, too, that self-employed individuals can create, with the help of a pension consultant and actuary, a special kind of retirement savings account called a defined-benefit plan. Using a defined-benefit plan, you may be able to contribute $50,000 or even $100,000 a year to a tax-deductible and tax-deferred investment account. And note that in these cases, as much as half of this money might be funded indirectly from federal and state income and payroll tax savings. For more information about a defined-benefit plan ask your tax advisor or attorney to refer you to an actuarial consulting firm or pension consultant.

You can probably slightly boost your interest rate, too. You definitely want to make sure your real rate of return is as high as it can possibly get, so you'll want to really watch things like mutual fund expense ratios. A mutual fund expense ratio shows the mutual fund's expenses as a percentage of the fund's values. Research shows that mutual funds with low mutual fund expense ratios tend to produce higher returns.

You might even want to invest more of your wealth in the riskier but potentially more rewarding small-company stock market. Small-company stocks are much riskier than large-company stocks—especially over shorter investment horizons like a few years or even a decade—but over long periods of time they probably also return around 12 percent annually. Note, however, that while the increased risk of investing in small-company stocks means that you might on average have a good chance of reaching a specific wealth target, this risk also means that there's a very good chance you won't achieve your wealth target within the desired time frame.

And note, too, that over shorter investment horizons, there's less time for your annual returns to "average out" to the average. Even over a ten-year investment horizon, there's a very good chance that your average annual return will be significantly more or significantly less than the historical average.

Another thing you can do is lower your sights. Rather than shooting for $1,000,000, for example, target $500,000 or $250,000. This means you'll live on less. Maybe you don't want to do that. But I'm just trying to outline all your options. And maybe what might work best for you is trying to accumulate $250,000 in investment wealth rather than $1,000,000, then semiretiring and getting some new, low-stress job—perhaps in a less expensive location.

Anyway, those are all the easy ways to slightly accelerate your investment wealth program.

If you want to do more than slightly accelerate your investment wealth program, however, what you need to do is jump-start your investment wealth program by investing a financial windfall. To do this, you need to find an extra $20,000 or $50,000 or maybe even $100,000 to invest immediately. What this windfall does is let you catch up on your savings. If your investment wealth plan requires you to invest $2,000 a year for forty years, for example, coming up with an extra $20,000 in effect puts you at the same place you would have been after eight years. Coming up with an extra $50,000 puts you at the same place you would have been after fifteen years. And coming up with an extra $100,000 puts you at the same place you would have been after twenty-three years.

The thing to notice about these numbers is that an initial lump sum can take the place of many, many years of saving. And that means that if you can come up with a lump now, or sometime shortly in the future, your investment wealth program can work over a much shorter period of time.

Of course, the big question is where do you come up with a big extra chunk of money? But lots of people, and especially mature readers who don't have several decades over which to leisurely acquire financial independence, often have the following windfall opportunities:

- Sell an expensive toy. Now, I know you don't call it a toy—and this is awkward for me, too—but do you have a boat or a motor home or a vacation home? Or how about an expensive piece of jewelry, some vintage musical instruments, or heirloom furniture? It's very possible you may be able to sell some personal item—especially if you've spent much of your adult life spending money instead of saving it—and then use this money to make up for the fact that you didn't begin saving earlier. As I talk to people, I learn that a surprising number of mature investors have property they could liquidate for handsome sums. It is not uncommon to have $20,000 or even $50,000 of money tied up in such items. Note, however, that if you do sell some item and enjoy a capital gain, you will need to pay capital gains taxes.

- Downsize your lodging. If you've got some big home in the suburbs—and especially if the kids are now grown—you may be able to free up a huge amount of money by selling the home and then moving to smaller quarters. A convenient condo, for example. Note, by the way, that most people can now avoid capital gains taxes on the sale of a home because there's a rule that says as of May 7, 1998, you can exclude up to the first $250,000 ($500,000 if you're married) of capital gain from the sale of a primary residence.

- Save any inheritances. Many people, and you may be part of this group, will receive substantial inheritances from their parents. You can't count on this, obviously. A parent may disinherit you. Or the expenses of a protracted illness or special care may erode the value of even substantial estates. But if you do receive an inheritance or you will receive an inheritance, you can vastly accelerate your investment wealth program by saving the money.

Let me make three final, quick comments about accelerating your investment wealth program. First, you can and should test the validity of this notion—that a financial windfall can accelerate your progress toward financial independence—by returning to the discussion of the Financial Independence Calculator in Chapter 1. All you need to do is add the windfall amount to the current savings input.

Second, Chapter 6 describes how you can use windfalls for contributing money to tax-advantaged investments like 401(k)s and IRAs.

Third, if you really can't stand the thought of working, and this is the reason you want to expedite your investment wealth program, maybe you've just got the wrong job. Maybe with a different job—one with less stress or more fun—the idea of working and contributing for a few more years wouldn't be so bad. Just an idea.

SO, STEVE, ARE YOU A MILLIONAIRE?

You know what? I wish I didn't have to answer this question. I grew up in a family where money was something you didn't talk about in public. But it does seem legitimate for you to wonder about this. We've spent a lot of time talking about you and your money. It's only fair to spend a few paragraphs talking about me. What's more, right or wrong, answering this question has become one of the things that the people who write books like this are supposed to do. So I will answer this question—although not before I explain why both the question and its answer are often misleading.

Okay, here's the reason: The fact that some author or seminar speaker is rich doesn't prove the author's or speaker's plan works. In many cases, the person has gotten rich selling people a get-rich scheme. And while the author's or speaker's wealth does prove that the person knows how to write a best-selling book or how to run a profitable seminar business, the wealth doesn't prove anything more than that. The wealth certainly doesn't prove that the get-rich scheme works.

This makes sense, right? Somebody who gets rich by, say, selling you a $200 book about investing in commodities or derivatives doesn't necessarily know how to become rich by investing in commodities or derivatives. He or she knows how to get rich by publishing $200 books. And there's a difference.

If you can't see the difference, remember that there are really three routes to wealth and that someone who gets rich from publishing books or speaking at seminars is taking the entrepreneurial route to wealth. They probably know an awful lot about that route. Their wealth does prove this. But they don't necessarily know anything about the other two routes. Maybe they do. Maybe they don't.

I hope you understand this. It's dangerously easy to get misled by people who know less than you now do about running an investment wealth program. Don't assume that because someone is rich that they have good investment advice.

And now it's time for me to stop procrastinating and to answer the question: Yes, I am a millionaire. More important, however, I possess a million dollars of net worth that directly stems from an investment wealth program just like the one I recommend you take. The major portion of this wealth is, predictably, money invested in tax-deductible, tax-deferred investment accounts like those described in Chapter 2. My own investment wealth program took roughly a dozen years to reach $1,000,000. While I didn't jump-start my investment wealth program, I should say that I enjoyed two unique advantages. First, I was self-employed and made rather good money. That meant I was able to use a SEP-IRA and contribute the maximum amount year after year. Second, I happened to invest in the stock market during a tremendously profitable period of time.

Epilogue

For almost two hundred pages, you and I have been talking about how you can map out a route to wealth. We're really done now. I've told you what you need to know: That an investment wealth program works and that all you typically need to do is make one or two smart decisions in order to get the ball rolling and to keep it rolling. Before we end our discussion, however, I'd like to share a couple of closing comments and make a request. And I'll do this stuff here.

A first closing comment: I want to emphasize one last time that running an investment wealth program isn't difficult. The only real tricks are to use tax-deductible, tax-deferred investment accounts, to invest your money in ownership investments, and to get whatever money you can't get from someone else by making a smarter decision or two. Perhaps the craziest part of all this—the stuff we've talked about through the pages of this book—is that getting rich and becoming financially independent isn't difficult. You just need to make a handful of clever decisions, and then you need to give yourself some time so that the compound interest engine can work its magic.

The real secret of wealth—if there is a secret—is that there are no secrets. While people spend all sorts of time chasing rainbows, trying new schemes, and attempting to outsmart the market, in the end, all it really takes is common sense and patience.

If you take nothing else away from your reading, therefore, know that running an investment wealth program isn't difficult. It isn't time-consuming. It's easy. A handful of clever decisions—that's all it takes. . . .

A second closing comment: While we've spent a bunch of time talking about how you can become financially independent, I want to repeat a point I made at the very beginning of this book: There's more to life than making and accumulating great gobs of money. Money doesn't make you happy.

What's more, the process of becoming financially independent is a housekeeping thing. It shouldn't become life's major activity. You spend a bit of time, perhaps a few minutes a day, working at it. And then you get on with the really important stuff: spending time with your friends and family, answering the big questions (like, "What's my purpose in life?"), and taking time to stop and smell the roses. You know all of this, I guess. So maybe what I'm really doing here is letting you know that I know this stuff, too.

Finally, I want to close this book with a request. I'd like to hear from you once you get going with your investment wealth program. Now, please don't send me a letter that says, ". . . and we're really going to start our investment wealth program next year. . . ." I don't want to hear that. In fact, I'm only going to get frustrated reading any letters like that. No, what I want to hear is that you've decided to run an investment wealth program using, for example, your employer's 401(k) and that you've already begun funding your investment portfolio by making a clever decision or two or maybe a small sacrifice. Maybe you've quit smoking or refinanced your mortgage or found ways to save money on your insurance. I want to know that you've already begun the journey— that you're already making steady progress down the road to financial independence.

If you find the time to write, please tell me, too, if there was something you read here that didn't make sense or wasn't all that helpful. It's always hard to receive criticism. And I'm as sensitive as the next writer. But I will truly appreciate your honesty.

You can send me any letters in care of the publisher. While I won't be able to respond individually to every letter, I will read each one.

Good luck!

Stephen L. Nelson

Seattle, Washington

March 1998

Appendix A
USING THE MILLIONAIRE MAKER SOFTWARE

In order to implement the investment wealth program described in these pages, you need to install and then use the Millionaire Maker software, which comes on the CD attached to the back cover. While this software isn't difficult to use or install, a bit of hand-holding is always comfortable. So I want to quickly describe how you install the Millionaire Maker software and then how you use it.

INSTALLING THE MILLIONAIRE MAKER SOFTWARE

How you install the Millionaire Maker software programs depends on the operating system your computer uses. If you're using a PC running Microsoft Windows, you follow one set of steps. If you're using an Apple Macintosh that's running the MacOS, you follow another set of steps. For this reason, first figure out which computer and operating system you'll install the software on—you should be able to do this by looking at the computer when it's turned on—and then follow one of the instructions sets listed below.

Insight

Installation on a PC Running Windows 95/98 or NT 4.0 or later

If your computer uses the Windows 95, Windows 98, or Windows NT 4.0 or later operating system, install the Millionaire Maker software by taking the following steps:

STEP 1   Click the Start button. This displays the Start menu.

STEP 2   Choose Settings to display the Settings submenu.

STEP 3   Click the Control Panel command to display the Control Panel window.

STEP 4   In the Control Panel window, double-click the Add/Remove Programs icon. This displays the Add/Remove Programs Properties dialog box.

STEP 5   Click the Install button.

STEP 6   Insert the Millionaire Kit CD in your CD-ROM drive and make sure you don't have a floppy disk in your floppy disk drive.

STEP 7   Click Next to have Windows search for a setup program. First Windows looks on your floppy disk drive. Then it looks on your CD-ROM drive. Windows won't find a setup program, so you have to click the Browse button to tell Windows where it is.

STEP 8   In the Look In drop-down list box, select the Millionaire Kit CD on your CD-ROM drive (this is probably your D: drive). When you do this, the list box displays two folders: Win3x and Win32.

STEP 9   Double-click the Win32 folder. The list box now has only one file in it, the Setup file.

STEP 10   Select the Setup file from the list box and click Open.

STEP 11   Click Finish to run the setup program.

Insight (continued)

STEP 12   Follow the onscreen instructions. Windows will install the Millionaire Maker software on your computer, creating a new program item on the Programs menu called Millionaire Maker. If you choose the Millionaire Maker item, you will see the Millionaire Maker menu. It lists each of the Millionaire Maker's software tools.

USING THE MILLIONAIRE MAKER SOFTWARE

You shouldn't have any serious trouble working with the Millionaire Maker software. As a general rule, all you do is start the program in the same way that you start any program. Then you fill in the blanks and click Estimate. The calculator then takes your inputs and works through the math to make some calculations.

If you do have trouble, click the Example button. When you do this, the program fills in the blanks for you with example data. What you can do in this case is then edit the data. In this way—by editing existing data that the program does understand—you're less likely to make a mistake.

If, perchance, your inputs don't make sense or aren't legible to the program, you'll see an error message on the screen. This doesn't happen often, fortunately. But it is possible. And I should say that if you enter crazy inputs or try to analyze some financial opportunity that is pretty wacky, the software tools can, basically, freak out. Say, for example, that you try to calculate the mortgage payment on a $150,000,000,000 mortgage. Or say that you try to use a calculator to analyze a loan that charges you 40 percent annual interest. These sorts of extreme financial conditions may sometimes push the calculators beyond their limits. And in these cases, you may also see an error message.

Insight

Installation on a PC Running Windows 3.0, 3.1 or 3.11

If your computer uses the Windows 3.x operating system, install the Millionaire Maker software by taking the following steps:

STEP 1   Start Windows in the usual way.

STEP 2   If necessary, display the Program Manager. Note that you may not need to do anything special to display the Program Manager. Windows may automatically display the Program Manager when you start Windows.

STEP 3   Insert the Millionaire Kit CD in your CD-ROM drive and make sure you don't have a floppy disk in your floppy disk drive.

STEP 4   Choose the File menu's Run command.

STEP 5   When Windows displays the Run dialog box, click the Browse button.

STEP 6   When Windows displays the Browse dialog box, select the Millionaire Kit CD on your CD-ROM drive (this is probably your D: drive). When you do this, the list box displays two folders: Win3x and Win32.

STEP 7   Double-click the Win3x folder. The list box now has only one file in it, the Setup file. Select the Setup file from the list box and click OK.

STEP 8   Click OK to run the setup program.

STEP 9   Follow the onscreen instructions. Windows will install the Millionaire Maker software on your computer, creating a new program group with program items for each of the Millionaire Maker's software tools.

Let me mention one other final point. Unless the book says otherwise or the calculator gives you the option, I generally assume that any stream of payments that occurs is an ordinary annuity. What this means is that I

Insight

Installing on an Apple Macintosh

If you're using an Apple Macintosh, install the Millionaire Maker by taking the following steps:

STEP 1   Start your Mac in the usual way.

STEP 2   Insert the Millionaire Kit CD in your CD-ROM drive.

STEP 3   Double-click the CD icon. You'll see the Millionaire Maker folder.

STEP 4   Drag the Millionaire Maker folder from the CD to your Mac's hard disk. Once you do this, you can start any of the Millionaire Maker programs by opening the Millionaire Maker folder you've just copied and double-clicking one of the programs shown.

---

assume any amounts you save, pay, or receive occur at the end of the month, year, or whatever—instead of at the end of the month. If some calculator is supposed to calculate the future value of your monthly 401(k) contribution, for example, I told the calculator to assume that you're making your monthly contributions at the end of the month, not the beginning of the month. What this ordinary annuity assumption means is that in the case where you instead make your save, pay, or receive month at the beginning of the month, year, or whatever, the calculator understates the interest you've earned or paid. Okay, I know this isn't perfect. What if you really make your payments at the beginning of, say, the year? Nevertheless, I had to make an assumption one way or the other in order to keep the calculators simple. And it seemed to me to make more sense to play it safe and err on the conservative side—which is pretty much what happens by going with the ordinary annuity assumption.

And now, all of that said, some people (and if I were a reader, I might find myself in this group) will get confused or befuddled when trying to work with a particular Millionaire Maker software program for the first time. So, let me provide some tips and point out some traps. I describe the Millionaire Maker calculators in alphabetical order.

ARM ANALYZER

The tricky part of looking at adjustable-rate mortgages, or ARMs, is figuring out whether you can stand the risk of having your payments increase because interest rates rise. If you've ever looked seriously at an ARM, you know what I mean. Is the lower starting interest rate on an ARM worth the risk that someday the payment may rise because interest rates rise?

While ARMs are tricky, you can gain quite a bit of insight into their true risk by comparing ARM payments to what you would pay on a fixed-rate mortgage and to your income. So, to let you think more objectively about an ARM, the ARM Analyzer compares what happens with an ARM in a worst-case scenario with rates rising every year with what happens if you have a fixed-rate mortgage. Then, to make this analysis more meaningful, the ARM Analyzer lets you estimate how your monthly wages will increase because of inflation.

The step-by-step instructions in Chapter 3 describe what each of the calculated numbers mean, but let me again point out that what you want to pay close attention to are the Income and Safe ARM % columns. The Income column shows how your income may grow if there's inflation pushing up the interest rates used to calculate your ARM payments. The Safe ARM % column shows what percent of your income you'll need to devote to make the suggested payment. The suggested payment is the greater of the required ARM payment or the "no-sweat" growing payment. The trick is to make sure that the actual ARM payment doesn't grow to some painful percentage of your income.

COLLEGE SAVINGS CALCULATOR

Even though the Millionaire Kit is really about achieving financial independence, I created a calculator you can use to figure out how much money you should be saving in order to pay for a child's college costs. The College Savings Calculator is described in Chapter 7. Look there if you have questions about how to use the College Savings Calculator.

COST OF HABIT CALCULATOR

The Cost of Habit Calculator, which is first described in Chapter 4, lets you calculate the wealth you give up because you make some habitual purchases. I talk about this calculator and its logic at several places in the book, so I won't repeat myself here. You don't want to hear me rail against smoking again anyway. But do note—and this is the last time I'll beat this drum—that it's easy to piddle away money you could instead use to fund a fortune.

EARLY LOAN REPAYMENT CALCULATOR

In Chapter 3, I pointed out that the true economic benefit of repaying some loan, such as a mortgage, early is often pretty slight. As Chapter 3 explains, while early repayment of a loan can seem like a wonderful investment, you typically build far more wealth by instead investing any extra principal payments in tax-advantaged investments. You can use the Early Loan Repayment Calculator to confirm this advice.

EASY LOAN COMPARER

I made this point in Chapter 3 when introducing the Easy Loan Comparer program, but small differences in interest rates can make a huge difference to your investment wealth program. If you can save just 0.25 percent—one quarter of one percent—on a $100,000 mortgage, your interest savings might grow to $100,000 in wealth by following the strategies described in Chapter 2. Unfortunately, it can often be tricky to figure out just which loan really is cheapest. And that's where the Easy Loan Comparer helps. It lets you figure out which of your loan options is cheapest.

Financial Independence Calculator

The Financial Independence Calculator is probably the most important tool in the Millionaire Kit. Too often, people talk about wealth building without ever concretely defining a goal. What the Financial Independence Calculator does is let you concretely define what "financial independence" means in your specific case. $1,000,000? More? $250,000? Less?

I actually spend quite a bit of time thrashing through the various steps in Chapter 1, which is where the Financial Independence Calculator is described. So you won't benefit by having me regurgitate that information again here. Nevertheless, let me make two quick points:

First, if you do have problems, you can click the Example button to get both example inputs and an example set of calculations. When you click the Example button, the calculator shows how things look for someone making $30,000 a year and just starting a thirty-year journey to financial independence. In this scenario, and assuming someone enjoys a 9 percent return but suffers from 4 percent inflation, the person needs to save $625 a month in order to accumulate $520,161.65 over the next thirty years. This wealth produces annual income of $26,008.08, which should provide for financial independence. Note that the roughly $520,000 of wealth and the roughly $26,000 of financial independence income use current-day, un-inflated dollars. You don't, therefore, need to adjust for inflation as you look at these numbers. The calculator has already done that.

Second, let me mention that you stick your existing investment portfolio balance—the amount of money you've already saved—into the Current Savings box. For example, if you've got $10,000 saved already, you plop 10,000 into the box. You stick the monthly amount you'll add to your investments into the Monthly Savings box. This may be beating a dead horse, but people sometimes get confused about what amount goes into what savings box.

HOME EQUITY LOAN ANALYZER

You can use the Home Equity Loan Analyzer, which is described in Chapter 4, to determine whether or not you save money by using a home equity loan to pay off your credit card and other expensive debts—usually you do—and to set a home equity loan payment amount that makes sense.

INVESTMENT CALCULATOR

The Investment Calculator, which is first described in Chapter 1, lets you make investment present value, future value, term, return, and payment calculations. Sometimes people also call these "five-key" calculations because with a hand-held calculation, you use the five financial keys. Unfortunately, unless you're comfortable using a financial calculator—if, say, you studied finance or accounting in college—you'll probably find the Investment Calculator a bit tedious to use. And, in fact, if you find yourself doing much head-scratching over it, I would recommend you not waste a bunch of time trying to figure a tool you'll need to use only once in a blue moon.

Instead, just carefully follow the step-by-step instructions provided in the pages of *The Millionaire Kit*. And then be done with it.

If you do need to use the Investment Calculator for other financial problem solving, let me make five simple suggestions:

1. Make sure you mark the correct option button in the Investment Variable to Calculate option button set. You mark the button that corresponds to the number you want to calculate.

2. Make sure you mark the correct option button in the Type of Payment Annuity button set. You mark the button that describes how

often you make or receive your regular payments. Note, too, that the calculator assumes the amount shown in the Regular Investment Addition box is paid or received at the frequency indicated in the Type of Payment Annuity button set. In other words, if you mark the biweekly button, the amount shown in the Regular Investment Addition box is a biweekly amount. And if you mark the annually button, the amount shown in the Regular Investment Addition box is an annual amount.

3. If you're using a Windows PC and, therefore, the Microsoft Windows operating system, you enter cash outflows (money you pay out) as negative numbers and enter cash inflows (money you receive) as positive numbers. Note that you interpret values that the program calculates in the same way. A negative number indicates you're paying the amount—that money is flowing out of your checking account or money market fund. A positive number indicates you're receiving some amount—that money is flowing into your checking account or money market. If you're using a Macintosh, by the way, you enter all the amounts as positive amounts and just interpret the amounts according to the context of the calculation.

4. If you can't seem to get the data entered correctly, click the Example button to have the program show you a sample calculation.

5. Finally, make sure that you enter the annual return on investment as a percentage. In other words, you enter a 10 percent return on investment as 10. You don't enter it as 0.10. You see the difference, right? You don't need to include the decimal point.

LIFE INSURANCE CALCULATOR

The Life Insurance Calculator, which is described in Chapter 5, lets you calculate how large a life insurance policy you need to replace the portion of your income that pays your family's living expenses. In other words, the Life Insurance Calculator figures out how much life insurance your family needs to stay afloat financially if you die. This is why, incidentally, the calculator adjusts your gross monthly income for any work expenses you now pay and any Social Security survivors' benefits your family receives after your death. Your family won't pay your work expenses after you die because you, obviously, won't be working. And Social Security may replace some portion of your income through survivors' benefits insurance.

The one thing you probably want to do when you work with this calculator is be conservative in your interest rate and inflation rate inputs. For example, even though the stock market earns perhaps a 10 percent return on average, you might want to assume that any life insurance proceeds would earn only 8 percent on average—perhaps because any amounts might be split between both stock and bond investments. And even though inflation over the last several decades has run at an average rate of around 3 percent, you might want to assume for life insurance purposes that it will run 4 percentage annually. This conservatism should cause you to overstate your life insurance requirements. But I think that's okay. To me, it makes more sense to provide your dependents with too much money than with too little.

LOAN CALCULATOR

The Loan Calculator, which is described in Chapter 7, lets you make loan balance, repayment term, balloon payment, interest rate, and payment calculations. While there's nothing intrinsically tricky about the Loan Calculator, unless you're comfortable using a financial calculator—if, say, you studied finance or accounting in college—you'll probably find the Loan Calculator a bit complicated. If I were you, I wouldn't waste a bunch of time trying to become some sort of Loan Calculator expert. Note, by the way, that *The Millionaire Kit* talks about the Loan Calculator only once and that's to walk you through the steps for figuring out what size loan payment you need to make in order to have a mortgage paid off by the time a child enters college.

In case you do want to use the Loan Calculator for other analysis, however, let me share several simple suggestions:

1. Make sure you mark the correct option button in the Loan Variable to Calculate option button set. You mark the button that corresponds to the number you want to calculate. Make sure you mark the correct option button in the Type of Payment Annuity button set. You mark the button that describes how often you make your regular loan payments.

2. Note, too, that the calculator assumes the amount shown in the Regular Payment text box is paid at the frequency indicated in the Type of Payment Annuity button set. In other words, if you mark the Bi-weekly button, the amount shown in the Regular Payment text box is a biweekly amount. And if you mark the Annually button, the amount shown in the Regular Payment text box is an annual amount.

3. If you're using a Windows PC and, therefore, the Microsoft Windows operating system, you enter cash outflows (money you pay out) as negative numbers and enter cash inflows (money you receive) as positive numbers. Note that you interpret values that the program calculates in the same way. A negative number indicates you're paying the amount—that money is flowing out of your checking account or money market fund. A positive number indicates you're receiving some amount—that money is flowing into your checking account or money market. If you're using a Macintosh, by the way, you enter all the amounts as positive amounts and just interpret the amounts according to the context of the calculation.

4. Finally, make sure that you enter the annual interest rate as a percentage. In other words, you enter a 10 percent interest rate as 10. You don't enter it as 0.10.

LOTTERY CALCULATOR

The Lottery Calculator, which is first described in Chapter 1, lets you simulate how a lottery works. You enter some inputs, including the payoff a winning lottery ticket pays, the price of a ticket, and your guess about the numbers. And then you click the Play Once button so that the calculator generates a random set of numbers just as the state lottery commission's computer does. If your numbers match the random numbers, you win.

To make the Lottery Calculator more useful, I added a Play 100 and a Play 1000 button. These buttons simulate what happens if you play the lottery 100 times or 1,000 times. My idea here was that by letting you play the lottery a bunch of times, you could get a gut feel for how your odds change if you can buy $100 or $1,000 or even $10,000 of tickets. (What you'll find, by the way, is that you still don't really have a chance in the standard lottery.) And that brings up a second point: I added counters that show how much you've spent on lottery tickets (since starting the Lottery Calculator program) as compared to how much you've won.

You can click the Play Once, Play 100, or Play 1000 buttons as many times as you want. For example, you can continue to click the Play 1000 button ten times in a row and thereby simulate what might happen if you bought 10,000 lottery tickets. But do note that your computer goes to quite a bit of work to generate the winning lottery numbers. So it may take a while to work through the calculations that simulate you buying one hundred or one thousand tickets. And if you do something like click the Play 1000 button several times in a row, well, you may just have time to go grab a cup of coffee.

Let me make one final, nit-picking point. In a real lottery, you get to pick as many sets of numbers and then you bet on one set of random numbers. The Lottery Calculator, for simplicity's sake, however, works backward. It lets you pick only a single set of numbers, but then lets you play the lottery multiple times with the same set of numbers simply by buying new tickets. This doesn't really matter or change the odds, however.

MORTGAGE REFINANCING CALCULATOR

As described in Chapter 3, the Mortgage Refinancing Calculator lets you determine whether you save money by refinancing a mortgage at some new, lower interest rate. You should be able to get the inputs describing your existing mortgage from your lender or even from the most recent loan statement. You should be able to get the inputs describing a possible new mortgage from the lender who will refinance your mortgage.

I said this in Chapter 3, but let me repeat a couple of important points here: To truly save money by refinancing you need to not use refinancing as a way to increase your borrowing via a larger loan. And you need to not use refinancing as a way to stretch out your loan payments over a longer repayment term.

RAINY-DAY FUND CALCULATOR

The Rainy-day Fund Calculator, which is described in Chapter 5, lets you estimate how large a rainy-day fund you should amass in order to pay insurance policy deductibles and to get through a period of unemployment or disability. You should be able to use this simple calculator without instructions, but you can refer to Chapter 5 if you do have questions.

SMART LEASE CALCULATOR

The Smart Lease Calculator, which is described in Chapter 4, lets you view a car lease as just another way to finance a car purchase—which in effect is what it is. You should be able to get all of the numbers you need for your analysis from the leasing company or the car dealer. Once you complete your analysis, you want to compare the implicit interest rate charged by the lessor—this is what the calculator does—to what the bank will charge on a loan to buy the same car. Then you pick the financing option—either the car loan or the car lease—with the lower interest rate.

SUPERCHARGED HOME ECONOMICS CALCULATOR

The Supercharged Home Economics Calculator, described in Chapter 3, lets you look at buying a home in pure financial terms. To do this, you compare what happens financially if you rent a home or apartment to what happens financially if you buy an equivalent home or apartment. In a nutshell, then, what you're trying to do is answer the question, "Does it really make good financial sense to buy a home or should I just rent?" The bottom line, so to speak, is the Profit (or Loss) from Home Ownership amount shown as the last line of the calculation. If this amount is positive, it means you make money by purchasing a home. If this amount is negative, it means you lose money by buying a home.

Of course, the tricky thing in using this calculator is coming up with all of the inputs. Note that most of these inputs you get from your research. In other words, once you start looking at homes to rent or buy, you should know what it will cost to rent a home and what it'll cost to buy a home. You can get the mortgage terms—interest rate, down payment, and repayment term—from a mortgage lender. (You can call someone in the Yellow Pages if you want.)

The remaining inputs are more difficult to gather, however. So let me provide three general tips:

1. If you click the Example button, you get a set of example inputs including many example percentages. For example, the example interest rate you'll earn is 10 percent, the example inflation rate is 3 percent, and the example selling costs percentage is 10 percent. In the absence of better numbers—say you're just starting your analysis—you can use any of these percentage inputs. I didn't just pick these numbers out of the air, in other words. I tried to use good, general averages.

2. Once you start working with a real estate salesperson or broker, you can ask them. Any experienced real estate professional will have good input regarding items such as property taxes, maintenance, and repairs. Note that a good salesperson should also be able to provide good input on the purchase closing costs in dollars and the selling costs percentage.

3. It's dangerous, in my opinion, to assume you will see year-in, year-out inflation of more than the historical average of about 3 per-

cent. You do yourself a disservice, for example, by assuming that even though inflation in recent history has been 3 percent, in the future it's going to steadily run at 6 percent. My concern here, by the way, is that if you overstate the inflation, you tend to overstate the benefits of home ownership.

Let me make one final point again even though I touched on this in Chapter 3: The Supercharged Home Economics Calculator ignores two important factors: the tax benefits of home ownership and the possibility that a renter may be able to direct savings into a tax-advantaged investment that includes employer matching [something like a 401(k) or Simple-IRA]. While I made this simplification in the calculator's operation to simplify your analysis, it turns out that this doesn't in practice mess up your analysis. I should say, however, that the calculator (because of these two simplifications) does tend to make home ownership look relatively better than it should—although only slightly. In other words, the calculator tends to be slightly prejudiced in favor of home ownership.

TAX ADVANTAGE ESTIMATOR

As described in Chapter 2, one of the basic points of the Millionaire Kit formula is that you can use tax advantaged investments to get much and sometimes even most of the money you need to build your wealth. People sometimes doubt this assertion. And that's really why I included the Tax Advantage Estimator calculator. It shows how much money you can get from your employer or from tax savings.

The one tricky aspect of the Tax Advantage Estimator concerns the marginal tax rate input. Your marginal tax rate is the total combined federal, state, and local income tax rate that you would have paid on the money you're not planning to divert to your investment wealth program. For example, if you're going to divert $10,000 to your investment wealth program—in other words, you're going to save this money rather than spend it—and you would have paid $3,000 in income taxes if you spent the money, your marginal income tax rate is 30 percent: $3,000 divided by $10,000 equals 0.3, or 30 percent.

Unfortunately—and I'm sorry about this—I can't tell you what your marginal tax rate is. You'll need to figure it out on your own by looking at your most recent tax returns. Nevertheless, let me point out that most people's federal marginal income tax rates are either 15 percent or 28 percent. In 1998, for example, someone who is single pays the 15 percent rate if their taxable income is less than roughly $25,000 and the 28 percent rate if their taxable income is between $25,000 and $62,000. And a married couple pays the 15 percent rate if their taxable income is less than about $42,000 and the 28 percent rate if their taxable income is between $42,000 and roughly $102,000. If your taxable income bumps above these amounts, you're a high-income taxpayer and so pay higher marginal rates of 31, 36, or even 40 percent. If you live someplace where you also pay state or local income taxes, you need to add the state and local tax rates to the federal rates in order to get your overall marginal tax rate.

TIMESHARE CALCULATOR

The Timeshare Calculator, described in Chapter 3, lets you look at buying a timeshare vacation property in terms of an equivalent nightly room charge. By doing this, you can get a better feel for what you're really signing up for. And you can ask yourself if you really want to sign up to pay, for example, $250 a night for your weekly vacations for the next twenty or thirty years.

Note that one really important variable in the Timeshare Calculator's analysis is what you ultimately sell the timeshare for. I set the resale value at 50 percent because when I visit resort areas, the people I talk with say you purchase resale timeshare properties at a 50 percent discount. But you'll want to validate this number by considering what the resale percentages look like in the area you're considering. By the way, if you don't have time to get this data and factor it into your analysis, you can't objectively assess a timeshare opportunity.

WEALTH ESTIMATOR

I included the simple Wealth Estimator program, which is described in Chapter 2, so that you have an easy way to prove the central premise of the Millionaire Kit—that an investment wealth program will produce substantial wealth. If you have questions about how to use this tool, refer to Chapter 2. But note that you can probably prove to yourself that the Millionaire Kit's formula works just by clicking the Example button.

WINDFALL CALCULATOR

The Windfall Calculator shows what happens if you take a financial windfall—say an inheritance or gift—and use it to fund investments. Note, by the way, that you get the biggest bang for your buck if you use a windfall to fund contributions to a tax-deductible, tax-deferred investment with employer matching. In this, you can easily double or even triple your money. For example, a $10,000 gift can be turned into $20,000 or $30,000 or 401(k) contributions, thereby jump-starting your investment wealth program.

One minor point: If you mark the Tax Deductible Yes button, the calculator marks the Tax Deferred Yes button and then disables the Tax Deferred button set. The calculator does this because if an investment is tax deductible, it is also by definition tax deferred.

Appendix B
HOW TO USE THE WEB GUIDE

The Companion CD also includes my own guide to the web's best personal financial planning resources. If you have a web browser (like Netscape Navigator or Microsoft Internet Explorer) installed on your computer, you know how to browse web pages, and you have an Internet connection, you won't have any trouble using the web guide. Just insert the Companion CD into the computer's CD drive. Then view the contents of the CD in the same way you'd look at the files and folders (or directories) of any other disk. When you see the file called Webguide, double-click it with the mouse to open it using your web browser.

An alternate way of opening the web guide is by opening your web browser first and then opening the webguide file using your web browser. For example, if you have Netscape Navigator, you would open the program, choose the File menu's Open Page command, and then click the Choose File button to locate the webguide file on the CD. If you have Internet Explorer, you would open the program, choose the File menu's Open command, and then click Browse buttons to browse for the webguide file.

Once you have the web guide displayed in your web browser, you can click a category at the top of the page to jump down to a list of sites within that category. To move to a site, just click its hyperlink.

Index